THE PANCAKE HANDBOOK

by
Stephen Siegelman
Sue Conley
and
Bette Kroening

Illustrations by
Mary Lawton

Ten Speed Press
Berkeley, California

🔟

TEN SPEED PRESS
P.O. Box 7123
Berkeley, CA 94707

Originally published by Oceanview Enterprises; this is a revised edition.
Cover design by Betsy Bodine Ford.
Text design by Fifth Street Design.

Library of Congress Cataloging-in-Publication Data
Siegelman, Stephen.
The pancake handbook / Stephen Siegelman, Sue Conley, and Bette Kroening.
    p.   cm.
    Includes index.
    ISBN 0-89815-593-2
    I. Pancakes, waffles, etc. I. Conley, Sue. II. Kroening, Bette. III. Bette's Oceanview Diner
(Berkeley, Calif.) IV. Title.
TX770. P34S54 1994
641.8 15—dc20   93-46566
                        CIP

FIRST PRINTING 1994

Printed in the United States
1   2   3   4   5   –   98   97   96   95   94

To the spice of our lives

Martin Lewis
Ranger Nan Haynes
Manfred Kroening
Graeme Mardon
Mike Ed Ford

Acknowledgments

*O*ur thanks to . . .

Frances Bowles for her skillful editing. Zelda Gordon for editing the original manuscript and for her insightful good humor. Phil Wood, George Young, Jo Ann Deck, Christine Carswell, Hal Hershey, Leili Eghbal, Lisa Ryers, and the staff of Ten Speed Press for all their help and hard work; Clifton Meek and the staff of Fifth Street Design. Everyone who contributed recipes to this book: Betty Groff (Groff's Farm Restaurant), Faith Stewart-Gordon and Loretta Debono (The Russian Tea Room), David Vardy (O Chamé Restaurant), Kaaren Erickson Sooter, Golda Meir, Ursula Kroening, Ellen and Philip Siegelman, Peg Smith (Chez Panisse Café), Niloufer Ichaporia, and Martin and Susan Yan. Natasha Dallin and Karen Rice, for their editing and friendship. Helen Gustafson, for her advice and support. Bambi McDonald, for proofreading and inspiration. And the staff of Bette's Oceanview Diner for their dedication to making and serving perfect pancakes.

Table of Contents

Bette's Diner, Berkeley, U.S.A.

*I*t's 6:00 a.m. in Berkeley, California, and already a line is forming in front of Bette's Oceanview Diner. It's been this way since we opened our doors more than a decade ago.

Those of us who started Bette's Diner back in 1982 are still a little in awe of this phenomenon. Even though we should know better by now, we still catch ourselves every so often wondering whether anyone is really going to show up. But every day they do: professors and poets, pundits and punks, students and starving artists, builders and businessmen, neighborhood regulars, and even tourists with maps, guidebooks, and reviews in hand.

It's an eclectic crowd, but after all, this is Berkeley, the birthplace of Free Speech and the epicenter of eclecticism. With their love of good food, strong coffee and lively conversation, our customers give new meaning to the term "counter culture."

Settle into a plush, red Naugahyde booth at Bette's and you're likely to be waited on by a cartoonist, a performance artist, a Doctor of Theology, or a rock musician. Drop a quarter in the jukebox and you can choose from the likes of Dolly Parton, The Meat Puppets, and Luciano Pavarotti. This is no ordinary diner.

The food has never been ordinary either. We look at it this way: A BLT is a simple, wonderful thing. But imagine a BLT made with thick applewood-smoked bacon, locally grown lettuce, juicy slabs of fresh tomato, and homemade mayonnaise on toasted rye bread from the bakery down the block. It's still simple. But it's *really* wonderful.

Now imagine an entire diner menu—from farm-style breakfasts to soups, salads, sandwiches, blue-plate specials, pastries and pies—all made from scratch with fresh, local ingredients.

And then there are the pancakes. Classic buttermilk pancakes have been a morning mainstay at the Diner right from the beginning. As their popularity grew, we added an array of daily pancake specials like blueberry buttermilk pancakes, sourdough pancakes, oatmeal pancakes served with chicken-apple sausage, cornmeal cakes with smoked pork chops, multigrain pancakes with fruit and yogurt, and buckwheat cakes with sour cream and caviar.

Not to mention crispy German-style potato pancakes with homemade applesauce. And our signature soufflé pancakes that emerge from the oven spectacularly puffed and golden brown.

A few years ago, a bit of good fortune literally fell at our feet. Someone on the staff found a box of paper coffee bags on the sidewalk in front of the Diner. We figured they must have dropped out of a passing delivery van. The box was undamaged, so we thought we might as well put the bags to good use. Before long, we had tested and hand-packaged our first pancake and scone mixes and began selling them out of our takeout shop next door.

Once again, we were a little overwhelmed by the response. We soon found ourselves with a second business on our hands: Bette's Diner Products. Today our mixes are selling like hotcakes in specialty shops and grocery stores all over the country. Like our pancakes at the Diner, our mixes are made with freshly milled flours and grains from a small, family-owned mill in San Francisco.

We've put together this pancake handbook so that you can enjoy our most popular Diner pancake recipes—along with a few of our favorites from around the country and around the world— at your place. We hope they have your friends and family lining up for more.

Pancakes Past & Present

*W*e pancake lovers like to think that the discovery of the pancake actually marked the very beginning of cooking. You see, pancakes date back to prehistory—probably even before the domestication of fire—when people first learned to mash grain and water together and bake the resulting dough on a hot rock in the sunshine. This was no mere gathering of food and cramming it into a hungry mouth. This was preparing and mixing ingredients, applying heat over time to effect chemical change, and winding up with an edible product that had never existed before. It was a great moment in anthropological history . . . and pancakes were there!

It's easy to imagine how those first unleavened breads were prized over other foods. It's believed that they held symbolic meaning to early sun worshipers because of their round shape and sustaining warmth. In making blini, which they ate throughout the long winter, the ancient Slavic people recalled the sun's golden image. In fact, there is evidence that pancakes were central to nearly all ancient cultures from Egypt, Greece, and Rome to Africa and China.

Today, pancakes remain one of the few foods universal to all cuisines, an Esperanto of the epicurean world. Some, like French crêpes and delicate Swedish pancakes, have long been familiar to American cooks. Others, like Irish potato boxty and Chinese onion cakes, are less well known.

The term *pancake* has come to mean a flat "quick bread," browned on both sides on a griddle. Basic pancake batter is made from flour and water or milk, maybe egg, maybe leavening, maybe sugar, honey or molasses, and maybe fat. In America, *pancake* generally refers to the classic white flour kind, often made with buttermilk. But this was not always so. The original American pancake was made from ground cornmeal by native Americans, who called it *nokehick*. It was introduced to European settlers in the early 1600s,

and its name was eventually corrupted into English as "no cake." This early American staple was often eaten three times a day.

In the 1700s, the Dutch added buckwheat *pannekoeken* to the American menu, and the English introduced the tradition of pancake feasts. These were held on Shrove Tuesday as a final binge before the deprivation of Lent. (Pre-Lenten pancake feasts and celebrations, which range from pancake-eating contests and flipping races to elaborate cooking competitions, live on in many parts of the world. The Sunday morning "pancake feeds" popular in churches throughout America are direct descendants of this tradition.)

By the 1800s, Americans had progressed from *no cakes* to *hoecakes* (thick cornmeal cakes so named because they were originally cooked on the blade of a hoe over an open fire by field laborers) and rice cakes made from milled rice flour. From Rhode Island came delicate cornmeal johnnycakes. Miners and lumberjacks in the Northwest favored sourdough pancakes made from a "wild" yeast starter. When provisions were in short supply, they invented thick and hearty flannel cakes (more colorfully known as sweat pads) made from stale bread soaked in milk.

With the current interest in regional American cooking, people are rediscovering all kinds of wonderful recipes and variations from our collective pancake past. We've included several in this book. Many are made with a variety of healthful and tasty whole grains, along with a few basic ingredients you probably already have on hand. We hope you have fun trying them, and that they inspire you to create a few pancake traditions of your own.

In Pursuit of the Perfect Pancake

Pancakes are simple food. They've been around for thousands of years, providing basic nourishment long before the invention of cookbooks and recipes and diners. So making pancakes should be simple, too. Even if you never cook, you can whip up a plateful of pancakes and sit down to a meal that's familiar, comforting, hearty, and healthy.

But then there are *perfect* pancakes—the kind you'd expect to find in the diner of your dreams. Perfect pancakes are something else altogether. They're steamy hot, light and fluffy, tender to the bite, yet hearty and rib-sticking at the same time. They're beautifully round and evenly risen, golden brown with delicate lacy edges, moist, rich, and slightly sweet with, perhaps, a hint of tangy buttermilk flavor.

When we opened Bette's Diner, we knew we wanted to serve nothing short of perfect pancakes. There we were on the first day, surrounded by all the right trappings: a sparkling stainless steel diner kitchen, a gleaming grill, thick restaurant china like the kind we remembered from the East-Coast diners of our childhood, little pitchers for the maple syrup, a batch of buttermilk pancake batter, and enough good intentions to pave a

highway. Our first pancakes were enormous, oblong, and flabby—a far cry from perfect. They came back half eaten. Someone in the kitchen dubbed them "heel pads," and we laughed gamely. But we were miserable.

"Heel Pads"

What we didn't fully understand is that there really are some basic principles that can elevate ordinary pancakes to "dream diner" material. These are not difficult principles, to be sure, but they're not immediately obvious, either. We've been collecting and refining them ever since that first day. Now, more than a decade and several hundred thousand pancakes later, we offer them to you in the spirit of Bette's Diner: Take something simple and make it the best it can be.

Picking Fresh Flours

*T*he more basic a recipe is, the more important it is to start with the best ingredients you can find. This is particularly true of pancakes. For starters, fresh eggs and good flour go a long way toward making better pancakes.

Although all-purpose flour makes a fine base for many pancake batters, it can become stale during lengthy storage in the warehouse, and contributes little in the way of flavor. Instead, look for higher-quality flour from a local or small mill. It's often sold in health food stores. Once you experience the difference freshly milled flour can make to the flavor and texture of pancakes and other baked goods, you'll never look back.

At the Diner we love to experiment with different grains and flours to create all kinds of signature pancakes. You can do the same thing at home. Unlike the batter for some baked goods, pancake batter tends to be forgiving; you can do a fair amount of tinkering without disturbing the balance of ingredients, particularly when it comes to flour. You can generally replace a quarter (and often up to half) of the flour in a given recipe with another kind with good results. Try substituting cake flour for some or all of the all-purpose flour in any pancake recipe. With its lower gluten content, cake flour helps make pancakes light and fluffy. Replacing a portion of the white flour in pancake batter with whole-wheat flour produces a rich, hearty pancake. Flours milled from grains other than wheat can add depth, color, and flavor to pancakes. Try substituting a small amount of rye, rice, buckwheat, or oat flour. (If you can't find oat flour, use quick-cooking oats, either whole or ground in a blender.) A tablespoon of wheat germ or cornmeal gives pancakes a delicately crunchy texture—and adds a little healthy fiber in the bargain.

Avoid self-rising flour, which contains added salt and baking powder—ingredients that should already have been included in your recipe.

Getting It Light

A good pancake, like a bad politician, is full of hot air. No matter the recipe, what makes all pancakes—and all baked goods—rise are bubbles of air trapped in the batter that expand during cooking. That's really all there is to the process of leavening.

There are three basic ways of getting air into batter: using yeast, folding in beaten egg whites, or adding baking soda (or baking powder). Although a few of the recipes in this book rely on yeast or beaten egg whites for leavening, most use either baking powder or baking soda. That's what makes them fall into the simple quick-bread family: They're easy to prepare, self-leavening, and ready to cook without kneading or rising, the moment you mix together a few wet and dry ingredients.

ABOUT BAKING SODA: Remember when your first grade-science teacher showed you how to make a "volcano" by pouring vinegar onto a little heap of baking soda? What was actually going on there was that baking soda (also known as bicarbonate of soda) was reacting with acid to form carbon dioxide. In pancakes and quick breads this reaction is used for leavening. Tiny bubbles of carbon dioxide gas are trapped in the batter as it bakes, causing it to rise. That's why when baking soda is used in a recipe, you'll almost always find an acidic ingredient, too, such as buttermilk, yogurt, vinegar, lemon juice, or even molasses. This liquid acidic ingredient starts reacting with the soda right away, so it's important to prepare and cook soda-based pancakes immediately before the batter goes flat.

ABOUT BAKING POWDER: In the late nineteenth century, someone had the bright idea of combining baking soda with powdered tartaric acid (cream of tartar) to create the one-step leavener now known as baking powder. When moistened, the tartaric acid dissolves and reacts with the soda. Recipes containing baking powder don't need added acids in the form of buttermilk, vinegar, etc. Double-acting baking powder (which is just about the only kind available in the United States) releases some gas when it is initially moistened and the rest when it is exposed to heat. This means that there's less urgency involved: You don't have to make the pancakes as soon as the batter is mixed.

Although baking powder contains a little cornstarch to absorb moisture and keep the soda and tartaric acid from reacting in the package, it does eventually go flat. It's a good idea to replace baking powder often–long before the expiration date on the package. You can test it by mixing a quarter teaspoon with one tablespoon of hot water. If the mixture doesn't begin to bubble immediately, replace your baking powder.

Our basic recipe for buttermilk pancakes (see page 34) uses both baking powder and baking soda. Why? At the diner, we need a batter that can hold up all day. That's where the baking powder comes in. But we also want the flavor and richness of buttermilk. That's where the baking soda comes in. Besides acting as a leavener, it also neutralizes the acidity of the buttermilk, eliminating much of its sourness.

Don't Batter the Batter

Have you ever noticed how pancake and quick bread recipes caution: "do not overmix"? If you want light, tender pancakes, don't take this advice lightly. Too much mixing overdevelops the gluten in the flour, making the batter elastic. Elastic batter means rubbery pancakes. Overmixing also bursts those precious air bubbles you've worked so hard to create. Without them, your finished product will give new meaning to the phrase "flat as a pancake."

Begin by thoroughly mixing the dry ingredients in their own bowl. This way, you'll need to mix the batter less once the wet ingredients are added. In a second bowl beat the eggs lightly (if the recipe includes eggs), then add the other liquid ingredients. If you're using melted butter, it's helpful to have the eggs and the other liquid ingredients at room temperature. If they're too cold, the butter will harden in clumps.

Add the dry ingredients to the wet ones all at once. Gently stir *just* until everything is moistened. Don't worry about the small lumps. They will cook out and disappear.

The Thick of It

*T*he consistency of pancake batter is important—and unpredictable. Your ingredients, how long you let the batter sit, and even the weather all contribute to the consistency of your batter. If the batter is too runny, it will spread out too much on the griddle, resulting in flat, thin pancakes. If it's too thick it won't spread properly and your pancakes may turn out doughy at the center. When the consistency is just right, the batter spreads in even rounds that rise and cook uniformly.

To thin pancake batter, start by gently stirring in a small amount of water or milk. Then try a test pancake and, if needed, continue to add liquid. Remember that batters made with wheat flour tend to thicken as they stand, so the longer you keep your batter around, the more you may need to thin it out.

Thickening batters is a little trickier because you need to be careful not to overmix them. Sift a small amount of flour over the batter, then gently fold it in. Or carefully incorporate a little wheat germ, quick-cooking oats, or granola.

Griddle Me This

*T*he classic sheet grill was once the centerpiece of the diner kitchen. Many short-order cooks still use it for scrambling eggs, making omelets, and cooking all kinds of hot entrées. At Bette's, we reserve the griddle for just a few items: home-fries, French toast, bacon, breakfast links, homemade scrapple, and, of course, pancakes. With its spacious, flat, evenly heated surface, there's nothing like a real griddle for creating perfect griddle cakes.

If you're lucky enough to have a stove with a built-in griddle, by all means, use it. If you really love pancakes, a small, free-standing electric griddle is a worthwhile investment. It lets you cook several pancakes at a time, heats evenly and is usually coated with a nonstick surface. Because it has a built-in thermostat, it doesn't require constant temperature adjustments. Cast-iron stovetop griddles—especially the ones that are designed to span two burners—also work well.

Needless to say, pancakes can also be made in a pan. If you have a large, well-seasoned, cast-iron skillet, you'll find it ideal for pancakes—thick enough to bake them evenly and keep them from burning on the bottom before they're cooked through. To clean the skillet between batches and to prevent sticking, rub it with a paper towel dipped in salt. To keep the pan seasoned, avoid cleaning it with soap or detergent and rub it with a little oil before storing. A pan with a nonstick coating can also be used for pancakes. Choose one with a thick, heavy bottom and as much flat cooking area as possible.

Easy on the Greasy

Even though they're made on a griddle or in a pan, the correct word for cooking pancakes is *bake*, not *fry*. Go easy on the fat you use to grease the griddle. Most pancake batters—all of the ones in this book—contain enough fat to prevent the cakes from sticking to the griddle. All that is needed is a light coating of vegetable oil, brushed onto the cooking surface with a paper towel. If your cooking surface is well seasoned or has a non-stick coating, you shouldn't need to keep greasing the griddle between each batch.

Unflavored nonstick cooking spray also works well for griddle greasing.

The Heat Is On

Like the consistency of the batter, the temperature of the cooking surface needs to be just right. Begin by heating the griddle or pan to low or medium. If you're using an electric skillet or griddle with a thermostat, set it to 375°F. Oil the surface lightly and heat for a few minutes, then test the temperature by sprinkling a few drops of cold water onto the griddle. If the water vaporizes immediately, the surface is too hot. If it boils and steams listlessly, it's not hot enough. When the droplets jump and dance on the griddle, you're ready to make pancakes.

Keep an eye on the temperature of the cooking surface, adjusting it as you go. Or as Bette says: "Fiddle with the griddle!"

Batter's Up!

At the Diner, we think that about a quarter cup of batter makes pancakes of the perfect size (about four inches). They cook evenly and are manageable to work with.

Gently pour pancake batter onto the griddle using a spoon, measuring cup, or, best of all, a quarter-cup (two-ounce) ladle, which lets you keep your hand a comfortable distance away from the heat. Hold the ladle just above the surface of the griddle. The higher you hold it, the more you risk breaking the air bubbles in the batter. Drizzling a stream of batter from on high like a Balkan waiter pouring tea makes for messy, misshapen pancakes. Spoon carefully, and the batter will spread out in perfect circles.

Don't let pancakes touch each other. Leave enough space between them so that they have room to spread out without merging. They'll cook better and look better. Don't move pancakes around while the first side is cooking. This breaks the seal between the pancake and the griddle, and the pancake will not brown as evenly or as thoroughly.

Flipping with Finesse

Flip pancakes when their surface is covered with bubbles and the edges look dry. This usually takes between two and three minutes from the time you pour the batter onto the griddle. Before you flip over to the second side, use a spatula to peel back a corner and make sure the first side is golden brown.

In cartoons, flapjacks are always cata-pulted sky-high off the griddle or tossed and flipped from a pan. It's dramatic, but nothing kills a pancake faster. Resist the temptation and instead slide a spatula under the pancake, turning it gently. Imagine you're flipping a fried egg and don't want to break the yolk.

After flipping, cook for a minute or two more. Never pat pancakes down with the spatula, and never flip them more than once.

Finishing Touches

How you present food is just as important as how you prepare it. At the Diner, we take a lot of pride in our presentations. Here are a few simple touches that can help make your perfect pancakes seem even more perfect.

- Warm everything–the plates, the syrup, even the room! Pancakes get cold quickly.
- Make pancakes all the same size–using a quarter-cup ladle will help–and stack them or arrange them in neat little rows.
- Pancakes are more attractive served first side up, because that side is more evenly browned.
- Top pancakes with a blob of whipped butter, warmed to room temperature and scooped out with a melon baller. Or serve a little pitcher of warm melted butter on the side.

- Add a simple garnish: a dusting of sifted confectioners' sugar, a sprig of mint, a few fresh berries, banana slices, or a wedge of orange. We like to garnish flavored pancakes with a little bit of the raw material that went into them: a few crisp slices of apple on apple pancakes, half a toasted walnut on walnut pancakes, and so on.

- Don't skimp on syrup. If you're serving maple syrup, treat yourself and your guests to the real, 100-percent pure variety. It's well worth the expense, and a little goes a long way.

- Serve pancakes with a selection of simple hot or cold homemade toppings. See pages 130-133 for ideas.

Keeping Pancakes Warm

*P*ancakes are at their peak when served steaming hot, right from the griddle. If you're a short-order cook, this is no problem. You plate them up, ring the bell, and they're on their way. However, if you don't want to be stuck in the kitchen while your friends and family gorge themselves on round after round of the pancakes you have worked so hard to perfect, there is another way.

Layer a few batches of pancakes on a cookie sheet lined with a cloth towel and keep them warm in a 250°F oven. Each layer should be separated from the next by a towel to absorb steam. Try not to stack too many layers. You can store pancakes in this way for up to ten minutes. As soon as the last batch is cooked, serve it first on a warm platter. This will start things off nicely. Then dish up your stored reserves, bring them to the table, and join the party.

With a little practice, you can keep two or three griddles or pans going at once, further speeding up the cooking process.

Another way to reduce the amount of time you spend in the kitchen is to do some advance preparation the night before. Though some batters hold well in the refrigerator overnight, most tend to thicken and lose some of their airiness. We feel that the best pancakes are made from batter that has just been mixed and allowed to rest for a few minutes. Instead of preparing the batter the night before, try measuring and mixing the dry ingredients in one bowl and the wet ones in another. Store the wet ingredients overnight in the refrigerator. It's a simple matter to combine the two mixtures just before cooking.

A Note on Nutrition

*A*re pancakes a healthy food? Absolutely. Current guidelines for healthy eating point to grains as one of the basic cornerstones of a healthy diet. And pancakes are rich in complex carbohydrates, the body's best source of energy. A hearty pancake breakfast does more than satisfy the soul. It can give you the fuel you need all morning long. And don't overlook pancakes at other meals. Add a simple savory topping or a side dish and they can make a wholesome, high-energy lunch or dinner, too.

It's the accompaniments that can turn a healthy pancake meal into an orgy of excess. If you're concerned about fat and cholesterol, try serving pancakes with fresh, healthy toppings, such as berries, sliced fruit, fruit compotes, or low-fat yogurt.

At the Diner, the words "no substitutions" have never appeared on our menu. We believe in staying flexible and encourage our customers to suggest substitutions and be creative. The same thing might be said for the pancake recipes in this book. There are all kinds of substitutions you can make to cut down on fat and cholesterol. Here are a few.

- Replace whole eggs with a cholesterol-free egg substitute or egg whites (two whites take the place of one whole egg).
- Replace melted butter with vegetable oil (canola oil is the lowest in saturated fat).
- Fruit purées can be used to replace fat in baked goods with surprisingly creditable results. Try replacing some or all of the fat in your favorite pancake recipe with applesauce. This works remarkably well in our basic buttermilk pancake recipe (see the low-fat variation on page 37).
- Use nonfat milk in place of whole milk or buttermilk— or substitute nonfat yogurt for buttermilk.
- Replace milk or buttermilk with fruit juice. Add a small amount of baking soda (about ¼ teaspoon).
- Use cholesterol-free cooking spray to grease your griddle or pan.

Of course, these substitutions will affect the flavor, texture and appearance of your pancakes. That's why, when all is said and done, we always come back to basic, classic pancakes, made with the kinds of fresh ingredients people have been using for centuries. Eat them in moderation as part of a varied, healthy diet and you're home free.

Pancake Mixes — A Mixed Bag

*P*ancake mixes are more than just a convenience food. What you're really buying in a good mix is a good recipe. What makes some mixes better than others? All good cooking begins with high-quality ingredients. Of course, being in the pancake-mix business, we like to think our Oatmeal, Buckwheat, and Four Grain Buttermilk pancake mixes are among the best you can buy. They're made from freshly milled flours and natural ingredients, and they taste like real, homemade pancakes should.

The problem with many pancake mixes is that they're made in giant batches with "over-the-hill" flour. The "just-add-water" variety tend to be made with powdered eggs and a variety of mysterious ingredients that wind up tasting less than fresh.

Multipurpose pancake/waffle/biscuit/dumpling/etc. mixes are convenient, but they promise too much. Have you noticed how everything you make from them winds up tasting more or less like a salty biscuit?

We've tasted just about every pancake mix on the market and found that the best ones are made by small mills or companies that buy from local mills. These mixes are designed to make pancakes, maybe waffles, and nothing more. They may be a bit more expensive and require a few extra steps and ingredients, but that's what makes them the best.

A Word about Waffles

Waffle batter is a lot like pancake batter, and it's a simple matter to turn many of the pancakes in this book into waffles. In fact, you'll find that our basic recipes for buttermilk, cornmeal, and buckwheat pancakes can all be used "as is" to make delicious waffles. If you're feeling adventurous and want to try making waffles from your favorite pancake recipes, you may need to make some modifications. Here are a few tips.

- You can increase the fat in a pancake batter by up to half. This keeps waffles from sticking to the iron and helps them brown.

- Try increasing the liquid slightly to thin the batter. A thinner batter spreads more evenly on the iron, and produces a more tender waffle.

- For lighter waffles, separate the eggs, beat the whites until they are stiff but not dry, and fold the beaten whites into the batter as a final step.

- For crisper waffles, add a small amount of sugar to the batter.

- To cook waffles, pour between half and three-quarters of a cup of batter (check the manufacturer's directions) onto the hot waffle iron, close the lid, and bake the waffle until it stops steaming and is nicely browned.

- Waffles freeze well, and frozen waffles can be easily reheated in the toaster or the oven.

The Pancake Pantry

*W*ith a few basic pantry staples, you can turn out most of the pancakes in this book without having to run to the store for special ingredients. Here's a checklist for stocking your pancake pantry.

Dry Goods
All-purpose flour
Whole-wheat flour
Buckwheat flour
Cornmeal
Wheat germ
Baking powder
Baking soda
Salt
Granulated sugar
Confectioners' sugar

Walnuts, pecans, or almonds
Dairy Products
Milk
Buttermilk
Butter or margarine
Eggs
Cottage cheese
Sour cream
Other Staples
Maple syrup
Vegetable oil

Judging by their ever-increasing popularity at the Diner, pancakes are making a major comeback. We think they deserve to. And we hope the recipes in this book will convince you to climb aboard the pancake bandwagon.

Perfect pancakes—unlike a lot of other things in life—require nothing more than a little practice and patience. Keep trying the same recipe again and again and pretty soon you'll have mastered something simple and satisfying that you can call your own. What could be more perfect than that?

Buttermilk Pancakes

Without a doubt, America's flapjack of choice is the good old buttermilk pancake. What follows is the buttermilk pancake recipe we've developed at Bette's Diner. These pancakes are sweet and cakey with a rich buttery flavor and appealing golden brown color.

If you find you don't have buttermilk on hand, use regular milk (see the recipe for Griddle Cakes on page 35). The pancakes will still be quite tasty, although a little less rich and fluffy.

Bette's Diner Buttermilk Pancakes

Besides being delicious, this recipe is extremely versatile. At the Diner, we use this basic batter to make all kinds of daily pancake specials.

Sometimes we mix ingredients into it before cooking. Or, easier still, we simply pour it onto the griddle, then sprinkle fruit, nuts or other ingredients right onto the pancakes before flipping them. If you have a family with diverse tastes or want to surprise your brunch guests with a variety of pancakes, this method can be very handy. Some of our favorite sprinkles and stir-ins include berries, sliced bananas, dried cherries, raisins, walnuts, and shelled sunflower seeds.

About 24 four-inch pancakes; serves 4

2 cups all-purpose flour	2 eggs
2 tablespoons sugar	2 cups buttermilk
2 teaspoons baking powder	½ cup milk
I teaspoon baking soda	¼ cup butter, melted
½ teaspoon salt	

In a large bowl, combine the flour, sugar, baking powder, baking soda, and salt. In another bowl, lightly beat the eggs, buttermilk, milk, and melted butter. Add the liquid ingredients to the dry ingredients all at once, stirring just to blend; the batter should be slightly lumpy.

Heat a lightly oiled griddle or heavy skillet over medium-high heat (375°F on an electric griddle). Portion ¼-cup measures of batter onto the hot griddle, spacing them apart. When bubbles cover the surface of the pancakes and their undersides are lightly browned, turn them over and cook about 2 minutes more, until the other sides are browned.

Following are some simple variations—all based on the preceding recipe—to get your creative juices flowing.

Buttermilk Waffles

This recipe, without any modifications, makes wonderful waffles.

For an extra light, crispy waffle, you can separate the eggs and beat the whites until they are stiff but not dry, then prepare the batter as directed, folding in the whites last.

Pour about ½ to ¾ cup of batter (check the manufacturer's directions) onto the hot waffle iron, close the lid, and bake the waffle until it stops steaming and is nicely browned.

Griddle Cakes

In place of 2 cups buttermilk and ½ cup milk, substitute 2 cups whole or 2-percent milk. Eliminate the baking soda and increase the baking powder to 1 tablespoon.

Fluffy Buttermilk Hotcakes

Separate the eggs and beat the whites until they are stiff but not dry. Prepare the batter as directed, folding in the whites last.

Crunchy Whole-Wheat Pancakes

Use 1 cup all-purpose flour and 1 cup whole-wheat flour; add ¼ cup toasted wheat germ.

Oatmeal Pancakes

Use 1¾ cups all-purpose flour and ¼ cup quick-cooking oats.

Bette's Blueberry Buttermilk Pancakes

To the batter, add 1 cup fresh, frozen, or drained canned blueberries and ½ teaspoon freshly grated orange rind. If using fresh berries, dust them lightly with flour to keep them suspended in the batter and prevent their color from running. Sprinkle the finished pancakes with confectioners' sugar and serve with whipped butter and Citrus Maple Syrup or Blueberry Compote (page 130).

Jane Lindeman's Lemon Blueberry Hotcakes

In place of 1 of the cups of buttermilk, use 1 cup lemon yogurt. Add 1 cup fresh, frozen, or drained canned blueberries in the batter, dusting fresh blueberries lightly with flour first.

Health Nut Pancakes

To the batter, add 3 tablespoons chopped, unsalted, toasted cashews, 2 tablespoons shelled sunflower seeds, 2 teaspoons toasted sesame seeds, and 1 teaspoon poppy seeds.

Darryl Kimble's Apple Pancakes

To the batter, add 1 cup diced, peeled tart apple (about 1 medium apple), tossed in 2 teaspoons sugar. Serve with Warm Apple-Currant Topping (page 131).

Butter Pecan Pancakes

Melt 2 tablespoons butter in a heavy skillet. Add ½ cup chopped pecans, 2 tablespoons sugar, and a few drops of lemon juice. Cook, stirring, for about 2 minutes, until the pecans are lightly toasted and the sugar is just beginning to caramelize. Cool slightly and stir the mixture into the batter. Serve the pancakes with warm maple syrup and butter.

Banana Upside-Down Pancakes

Slice three ripe bananas, crosswise, to make ⅛- to ¼-inch thick disks; toss the banana slices with 2 tablespoons sugar. Grease the griddle well. For each pancake, place 4 or 5 banana slices directly on the griddle in a circle slightly smaller than your finished pancake will be; immediately pour ¼ cup batter over the bananas to cover them. Cook as directed in the basic recipe. When you flip these pancakes, the sugared banana slices will be faceup and will have become deliciously and attractively caramelized.

Banana Rum Walnut Pancakes

To the batter, add 2 tablespoons dark rum, 1 cup mashed, very ripe bananas, and ¼ cup chopped toasted walnuts. Serve with warm maple syrup and butter.

Bacon Breakfast Cakes

Cook crisp, drain, and crumble 4 slices of bacon; add to the batter. Serve pancakes in stacks of two, topping each stack with a fried egg.

Strawberry Short Stack

Toss 1 cup sliced strawberries with 1 tablespoon sugar. Place strawberry slices on half-cooked pancakes just before flipping. Sprinkle the finished pancakes with confectioners' sugar and serve with whipped cream and additional sliced strawberries.

Low-fat Pancakes

In place of ¼ cup melted butter, use ¼ cup applesauce.

Corn Pancakes

*C*orn was a New World discovery, brought back to Europe from the Aztec tribes of Central America. But as the centuries passed, corn never quite caught on in Europe as it has in North America.

In France and Italy, no one eats corn on the cob—it's thought of as uncouth. Whole kernels can be found in some vegetable dishes, but most fresh corn is reserved for feeding cattle and geese. Instead, corn is seen as a grain, best suited to drying, grinding into a meal, and cooking as a mush, the most famous of which is polenta.

There's no food more American than corn. And cornmeal pancakes—with their heavenly combination of delicate, crunchy texture and sweet, substantial flavor—have evolved as a uniquely American specialty.

Cornmeal, ground from dried corn kernels, is available in three textures: fine, medium, and coarse. At the Diner, we use fine stone-ground (also known as water-ground) cornmeal. It's milled the old-fashioned way, between water-powered stone grinding wheels, a process that preserves some of the hull and germ of the corn. The result is a nutritious product with a rich, nutty, whole-grain flavor. Most major commercial brands of cornmeal today, on the other hand, are steel-cut. This process strips away almost all of the germ and husk, breaks down the natural fiber of the corn, and reduces the nutritional value and flavor. Stone-ground cornmeal can be found in health food stores and some supermarkets. It's worth tracking down.

Cornmeal comes in three colors — yellow, white, and blue — depending on the type of corn from which it was made. At Bette's, we generally use yellow cornmeal. It tends to be more flavorful than white cornmeal, and we like the bright color it brings to the plate.

Bette's Diner Cornmeal Pancakes

These pancakes are the star attraction of our Virginia Breakfast: three corn cakes, a grilled smoked pork chop, and custardy scrambled eggs. They're light and sweet with a tender crunch. Be sure to use fine *cornmeal.*

About 20 pancakes; serves 4

2 cups water
2 tablespoons butter, plus extra
   for serving
1 cup fine yellow cornmeal
¼ teaspoon salt
1 tablespoon sugar
2 eggs

½ cup milk
¼ cup whole-wheat or
   all-purpose flour
¼ cup cake or all-purpose flour
2 teaspoons baking powder
Warm maple syrup

In a small saucepan, bring the water and butter to a rolling boil.

In a large bowl, combine the cornmeal, salt, and sugar. Pour the boiling water and butter over the cornmeal mixture and stir to combine. Cover the bowl (use plastic wrap or a clean kitchen towel) and let it sit for 10 minutes.

In a separate bowl, beat the eggs and milk together. Add the flour and baking powder. Mix lightly. Add the egg mixture to the cornmeal mixture, stirring gently just to combine.

Heat a lightly oiled griddle or heavy skillet over medium-high heat (375°F on an electric griddle). Portion ¼-cup measures of batter onto the hot griddle, spacing them apart. When bubbles cover the surface of the pancakes and their undersides are lightly browned, turn them over and cook for about 2 minutes more, until the other sides are browned. Serve immediately with butter and warm maple syrup.

Fresh Corn Pancakes

To the basic batter, add ½ cup uncooked, fresh sweet corn kernels.

Cornmeal Waffles

This recipe, without any modifications, makes outstanding waffles. For an extra light, crispy waffle, you can separate the eggs and beat the whites until they are stiff but not dry, then prepare the batter as directed, folding in the whites last. (You can add ½ cup uncooked, fresh corn kernels to this batter, too.)

Pour about ½ to ¾ cup of batter (check the manufacturer's directions) onto the hot waffle iron, close the lid, and bake the waffle until it stops steaming and is nicely browned.

Lacy Johnny Cakes

Cornmeal pancakes got their start in the South as hoecakes (originally cooked right on the blade of a hoe over an open fire) and corn pone—both eggless quick breads made by frying or baking patties of cornmeal mush. Corn cakes headed north in the early 1700s, when Rhode Islanders began using heart-shaped cast-iron griddles heated over the hot coals of an open fire to cook thick cornmeal patties called johnny cakes.

Pancake scholars continue to debate the origins of this name. It may have come from "journey cakes" (the hearty cakes were great road food), "Shawnee cakes," or even a corruption of the Dutch, pannekoeken. In any event, Rhode Islanders take the matter seriously. The use of white or yellow cornmeal, eggs, water, and scalded milk are all hotly contested, and there's even a Society for the Preservation of Johnnycake Tradition. Two warring camps have arisen: one side spells "Johnny" with the "h," the other without. The subject has even been debated on the floor of the state legislature. But then, Rhode Islanders call milk shakes "cabinets," so their language appears to have a logic of its own.

We've invented our own version. The batter is thinner than most, and the pancakes spread quickly on the griddle. You'll see why we call them "lacy." As they cook, they become covered with tiny bubbles. These pancakes cook quickly, so be prepared to stand by the stove. They're delicious on their own with maple or fruit syrup, or served with ham and eggs.

About 32 pancakes; serves 4

2 cups milk	½ teaspoon salt
1 cup fine yellow cornmeal	2 eggs, lightly beaten
6 tablespoons butter, melted	2 teaspoons vegetable oil,
2 tablespoons sugar	for frying

In a small saucepan, scald the milk by heating it just below the boiling point; remove from the heat. Place the cornmeal in a bowl and pour in the scalded milk. Stir lightly to combine. Cover the bowl with a clean kitchen towel and let the mixture sit for 10 minutes. Stir in the melted butter, sugar, salt, and beaten eggs.

Lightly grease the griddle with vegetable oil and heat it to medium-high. Pour the batter by tablespoonfuls onto the griddle.

The batter will spread quickly and should sizzle immediately, forming tiny bubbles. Flip after 30 seconds or when bottoms are nicely browned. Cook for 30 seconds more on the other side.

Groff's Farm Corn Fritters

*T*his recipe comes to us by way of another Betty—Betty Groff, the chef and owner of Groff's Farm Restaurant in Mount Joy, Pennsylvania, the heart of Amish country. She's been serving these silver-dollar-sized corn fritters in her restaurant for more than thirty-three years. Betty grows her own sweet corn and freezes hundreds of quarts of it each summer for use all year.

"Some people make corn fritters by deep frying a heavy biscuit batter with a little corn in it," says Betty. "Our fritters are made the traditional Pennsylvania Dutch way. They're mostly good sweet corn, browned in a little butter. We keep it simple so the flavor of the corn can really come through."

These are perfect for breakfast or as a summertime vegetable side dish.

About 16 three-inch fritters; serves 4

1½ cups fresh sweet corn
    kernels (about 3 ears of
    corn) or 1 can (17 ounces)
    sweet corn, drained
2 eggs

2 tablespoons all-purpose flour
½ teaspoon salt
⅛ teaspoon ground pepper
½ teaspoon sugar
⅓ cup butter

Place all the ingredients except the butter in a blender or food processor. Cover and blend for about 15 seconds until the ingredients are thoroughly combined.

In a large, heavy skillet, heat some of the butter over medium heat. Drop the batter by tablespoonfuls into the hot butter. Fry until the fritters are nicely browned, about 3 minutes on each side, adding butter to the skillet as needed. Serve with light molasses or maple syrup.

46

Buckwheat Pancakes

*D*espite its name, buckwheat bears no relation to wheat. In fact, even though it's cooked as a cereal and ground to make flour, buckwheat is actually not a grain at all, but a wild herb—a distant cousin of rhubarb—native to Russia and Central Asia. It was introduced to the West in the Middle Ages by Dutch traders who are believed to have named it *boek weit*, or "book wheat," a reference to the Bible. Buckwheat caught on in Europe because it is practically indestructible and can be grown even in poor soil with little effort. Amateur farmers were once known as buckwheaters.

The seeds of the buckwheat plant are ground to make buckwheat flour or are hulled and crushed to make groats, also known as *kasha*. Buckwheat flour is of little value in bread baking because it lacks gluten, but it does make outstanding pancakes with a distinctive tangy flavor. In fact, it's thought of primarily as a pancake flour by cooks all over the world, and turns up in everything from Russian *blini* to the *galettes* of Brittany.

Buckwheat is a naturally healthy food. Because it's a hearty plant, it has traditionally been grown organically without pesticides. It's also the best-known source of complex carbohydrates and is nearly a complete protein, offering more than 80 percent of the protein of eggs with no cholesterol or fat. And it's ideal for people on wheat-free diets.

Buckwheat flour isn't usually used alone in pancakes, because it tends to make them too thick and heavy. But in combination with wheat flour and beaten egg whites, yeast, or other leavening agents, it can produce a wonderfully soft, silky batter and fluffy pancakes that rise delicately from the griddle.

Bette's Diner Buckwheat Pancakes

Buckwheat cakes are a Wednesday special at the Diner. We serve them with pepper-cured bacon, eggs any style, and a pitcher of Vermont maple syrup. They're also delicious with fresh fruit and yogurt.

If you're having trouble finding a store that carries buckwheat flour or you don't want to bother keeping buttermilk on hand, you can always save a step and buy a bag of Bette's Diner Buckwheat Pancake and Waffle Mix. But if you've got the time and the ingredients, here's the secret formula.

About 16 four-inch pancakes; serves 2 to 4

½ cup all-purpose flour
½ cup buckwheat flour
1½ teaspoons baking powder
1½ teaspoons sugar
½ teaspoon baking soda

½ teaspoon salt
1 egg
1 cup buttermilk
¼ cup water
2 tablespoons butter, melted

In a large bowl, combine the flours, baking powder, sugar, baking soda, and salt. Separate the egg and, in a small bowl, beat the white until it forms soft peaks. In another bowl, combine the yolk, buttermilk, water, and melted butter; add this mixture to the dry ingredients all at once, stirring just to blend. Gently fold the egg white into the batter.

Heat a lightly oiled griddle or heavy skillet over medium-high heat (375°F on an electric griddle). Portion ¼-cup measures of batter onto the hot griddle, spacing them apart. When bubbles cover the surface of the pancakes and their undersides are lightly browned, turn them over and cook for about 2 minutes more, until the other sides are browned. Serve immediately with butter and warm maple syrup.

Buckwheat Waffles

Without any modifications, our recipe for buckwheat pancakes makes outstanding waffles. Pour about ½ to ¾ cup of batter (check the manufacturer's directions) onto the hot waffle iron, close the lid and bake the waffle until it stops steaming and is nicely browned. Serve with fruit syrup, maple syrup, or fruit and yogurt.

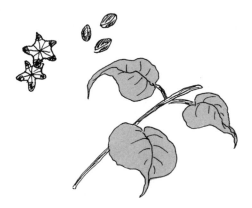

Blini

When we cater parties, we often serve our buckwheat pancakes (page 50) as a fancy finger food. We make them the size of silver dollars and top them with sour cream and caviar or smoked salmon—our version of blini, the elegant Russian buckwheat pancake.

Real blini are a bit more complex because they're made with yeast, which gives them a slightly sour flavor and an addictively light texture. They're well worth the effort.

Our favorite blini recipe comes from the "mother church" of Russian cooking in America, the Russian Tea Room, the opulent New York restaurant that has attracted artists, celebrities, and blini-lovers since 1926. The recipe below and its introduction are reprinted, with permission, from The Russian Tea Room Cookbook by Faith Stewart-Gordon and Nika Hazelton (Putnam, N.Y.: GD/Pedigree, 1981).

Russian Tea Room Blini

The ancient Slavic people worshipped the sun, hoping it would return and rescue them from the cold darkness of winter. They recalled the sun's golden image by making blini, little round pancakes, which they ate to keep warm. The week before the long seven-week Lenten season began was called Myaslanitza, or Butter Week, when everyone gorged on blini and other dairy products, which they then had to give up until Easter. We still have the Blini Festival every year at the Russian Tea Room to celebrate this winter-solstice event.

About 36 four-inch blini; serves 6

1⅓ cups sifted all-purpose flour	½ teaspoon salt
1⅓ cups sifted buckwheat flour	2⅔ cups milk
4 teaspoons active dry yeast	½ cup butter, cut into small
¼ cup sugar	pieces
	4 eggs, lightly beaten

In a large bowl, combine the flours, yeast, sugar, and salt. In a small, heavy saucepan, combine milk and butter. Heat mixture over low heat only until milk is warm (105° to 115°F) and the butter has melted. Stir frequently to speed up the melting of the butter; the milk must not be hotter than the temperature given above. Stir milk mixture into flour mixture and mix well; then stir in the eggs. Using an electric mixer at low speed, beat for about 1 minute or until smooth, occasionally scraping the sides of the bowl. Or do this by hand, beating energetically for 3 to 5 minutes. Cover bowl. Set to rise in a warm place for 1 to 1½ hours, or until mixture is about doubled in volume and light and bubbly. Preheat a griddle or a large (10-inch), heavy (preferably nonstick) frying pan. Lightly brush with a very small amount of melted butter. (Do not use too much, or *blini* will turn gray in cooking. The bottom of the griddle or frying pan should be covered with a very light film of butter.) The griddle or frying pan will be hot enough when a drop of water dropped on its surface will evaporate instantly. Stir down batter. To make 4-inch *blini*, spoon about 3 tablespoons batter onto the griddle or frying pan. Cook for 40 to 60 seconds or until the top is bubbly and the bottom browned. Turn over with a large spatula, or flip over, and cook for 30 seconds on the other side or until browned. Stack cooked *blini* on a heated serving dish and keep warm in a low oven (150° to 175°F).

Serve with a bowl of melted butter and a bowl of sour cream at room temperature, and with caviar or smoked fish such as salmon. To eat, brush butter on *blini* and top with a small mound of caviar or smoked fish. Top with a spoonful of sour cream and roll up.

O Chamé Buckwheat Shrimp Cake

Buckwheat plays an important role in the Japanese diet, and this Japanese-inspired recipe comes from our neighbor across the street, a remarkable California-Japanese tea room called O Chamé. Owner David Vardy serves light dishes of Zen-like simplicity, made with fresh, local ingredients—all designed to go well with tea.

    This delicately crunchy buckwheat and shrimp pancake is easy to prepare. It makes a nice small meal for one person or an appetizer for two to four. David serves it with a wonderfully creamy and flavorful soy-ginger dressing. He recommends a good oolong tea as an accompaniment.

I ten-inch pancake; serves 2 to 4 as an appetizer

2 eggs	9 medium uncooked shrimp,
¼ cup 100-percent malt beer	peeled, deveined, and
¼ teaspoon sea salt	chopped (to make about
2 tablespoons buckwheat flour	½ cup)
I tablespoon all-purpose flour	2 tablespoons vegetable oil
⅓ cup diced celery	

Beat the eggs lightly with the beer and salt. Gradually add the flours, mixing just to combine. Stir in the celery and shrimp.

    Heat the oil in a 10-inch nonstick frying pan over medium-high heat. Pour in the batter all at once and spread it in the pan in an even layer. When the underside of the pancake is nicely browned, flip the pancake and cook it for a few minutes more until the second side is brown and the center is set.

    Slide the pancake onto a plate and cut it into eight wedges. Serve it with soy sauce or Soy-Ginger Dressing.

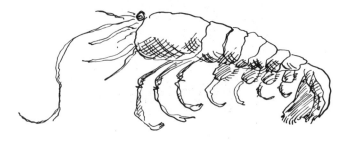

Soy Ginger Dressing

About 1 cup

1 egg yolk	1 ½ teaspoons Japanese-style
1 teaspoon lemon juice	rice vinegar
½ teaspoon dry mustard	¼ teaspoon fresh ginger juice
¾ cup peanut oil	(see box)
1 ½ teaspoons soy sauce	1 to 2 teaspoons water

In a small bowl, beat the egg yolk briefly with the lemon juice and mustard, using a whisk or electric mixer. Begin adding the peanut oil, a few drops at a time, whisking constantly so that each addition of oil is completely incorporated before the next is added. Once half of the oil has been added by drops, whisk in the remaining oil in a slow, steady stream. Whisk in the soy sauce, ginger juice, and vinegar. Thin the dressing by whisking in water, a few drops at a time, as needed, until the dressing has the consistency of heavy cream.

GINGER JUICE
*Make ginger juice by squeezing chunks
of fresh ginger through a garlic press
or by pulverizing them in a food processor.
Press the resulting pulp through a strainer.*

Crêpes

*C*rêpes are an international street food. Parisians make a quick meal of them at tiny food stands, where the fillings range from ham and Gruyère cheese to jam, Grand Marnier liqueur, or the elegantly simple *crêpe nature* rolled in butter and vanilla sugar. In Brittany, crisp, hearty buckwheat crêpes are filled with seafood and other savory and sweet fillings. The Russians fill their *blinchiki* with a cottage cheese or fruit stuffing. In Italy, delicate *crespelle* are rolled around savory meat or cheese fillings. And in Hungary, *palacsintas* are an everyday food served even in the humblest of households.

Somehow, Americans have come to view crêpes as a fancy delicacy. Don't be intimidated. Crêpes are a delicious treat, and they're not hard to master. They're really nothing more than paper-thin pancakes made of flour, milk, eggs, and butter. The batter is poured sparingly into a pan and cooked quickly.

Unlike classic pancake batter, crêpe batter needs to be beaten so that the gluten in the flour develops (a blender works well for this). It should then be chilled for an hour or more to allow the gluten to relax. The best crêpes are strong enough to hold a loose filling while still remaining soft and tender to the bite. They are served rolled, folded, or stacked.

The best tool for making crêpes is a French-style crêpe pan—a flat iron or steel pan measuring about six inches across the bottom and with low sloping sides, lightweight enough to be easily turned as you pour in the batter. A heavy nonstick pan can also be used. At the Diner, we've been using the same set of inexpensive French steel omelet pans for more than ten years. They stay seasoned, never stick, and are light and easy to hold.

Crêpe batter should be about the consistency of buttermilk, just thick enough to coat the ladle. Your first crêpe is likely to be a throw-away tester that will tell you whether your batter is thin enough (if it's not, add a little cold water) and whether the pan is hot enough.

As with most pancakes, the first side of the crêpe to be cooked is more evenly browned and attractive than the second, so you'll generally want to roll or fold crêpes with the first side facing out.

Crêpes can be made ahead of time, stacked, wrapped in plastic wrap and stored for up to forty-eight hours at room temperature or in the refrigerator. They can also be stacked between layers of waxed paper, wrapped in foil, and frozen.

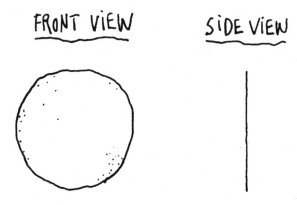

FRONT VIEW   SIDE VIEW

Crêpes are extremely thin.

Bette's Diner Crêpes

This basic crêpe batter works well for both sweet and savory fillings. Made in a blender, it's quick to prepare in advance.

At Bette's, we mainly use these crêpes to make blintzes (see page 80), cooking them on one side only, then rolling them around a cottage cheese filling with the uncooked side facing out. With six pans fired up at once, one cook can turn out fifty or more blintz wrappers in just twenty minutes. It's quite a sight. We make these at night for the following morning, turning them out onto cotton towels, then stacking them as they cool.

12 to 16 seven-inch crêpes

³/₄ cup cold water
¹/₂ cup cold milk
2 eggs

4 tablespoons butter, melted
¹/₂ teaspoon salt
I cup all-purpose flour

Place all ingredients, in the order listed, in a blender. Blend at top speed for about 30 seconds. Scrape down lumps from the side of the blender container with a rubber spatula. Blend for 15 seconds more. (If you don't have a blender, combine all the ingredients in a bowl and beat with a wire whisk or electric beater until well blended.) Cover and chill the batter for at least I hour.

Heat a crêpe pan over medium heat and wipe it with oil. Spoon in enough batter to barely cover the pan, tilting the pan to coat the bottom and part way up the sides evenly. Turn the crêpe over when the edges begin to pull away from pan and the bottom is lightly browned, I to 2 minutes. Continue cooking to brown the other side lightly, about 30 seconds more. Remove the crêpe from the pan and repeat the process, oiling the pan as needed and stacking the cooked crêpes.

Dessert Crêpes

Crêpes Nature

The simplest and most delicate of crêpe desserts. Prepare crêpes as directed on page 61. Place one cooked crêpe, with the second side facing up, back in the crêpe pan over medium heat to warm it briefly. Brush the surface with ½ teaspoon softened butter and sprinkle it with ½ teaspoon vanilla sugar (see box). Fold crêpe in quarters with the first side facing out. Sprinkle with a little additional vanilla sugar. Serve on warm plates, allowing 2 crêpes per serving.

VANILLA SUGAR

Split a vanilla bean lengthwise and place it in an airtight container with a cup of sugar. Remove the vanilla bean after one week and reserve it for another use. The sugar will be deliciously perfumed and flavorful. In a pinch, you can also make vanilla sugar by thoroughly combining 1 cup sugar with ½ teaspoon pure vanilla extract.

Coconut "Fancakes"

When Steve was a kid, his family spent a year in India. Their cook, Muragesan, was wonderfully inventive, working southern Indian ingredients into the French cuisine he had picked up while cooking for diplomats. Among his finest East-West creations were delicate coconut crêpes, which he called coconut "fancakes," named not for their fanlike shape but because Muragesan could not pronounce the letter "p," (he also made a delicious "phoenix" pudding from ground peanuts).

Prepare crêpes as directed on page 61. Sprinkle them with fresh lime juice and toasted, sweetened shredded coconut. Fold into quarters and dust with confectioners' sugar.

Sundae Crêpes

Fold two crêpes into quarters and place them, slightly overlapping, on a plate; top with a scoop of vanilla ice cream and some hot fudge sauce. Sprinkle with toasted sliced almonds.

Jam Crêpes

Spread crêpes with jam, roll up, and eat. Kids love these. Along these same lines, chocolate and nut butter (such as Nutella) or chestnut butter also make delicious fillings for warm crêpes.

Savory Crêpes

You can fill crêpes with just about anything. They take particularly well to creamy fillings, like creamed mushrooms, spinach, seafood, or chicken. They're also delicious filled with diced ham and Gruyère cheese, asparagus, *ratatouille*, goat cheese, or herbed cream cheese. Anything that makes a good filling for an omelette will work well when rolled into a crêpe.

You can prepare most filled or rolled crêpes ahead of time, arranging them in a single layer in a buttered baking dish. Reheat them in a 350°F oven until they have begun to brown lightly and are warmed through, 10 to 15 minutes.

Suzette's Crêpes Suzette

C rêpes Suzette is the showgirl of the pancake family. Drenched in a luxurious orange butter sauce and flambéed dramatically at the table, Crêpes Suzette was the elegant dessert in "continental" restaurants of the fifties and sixties. Nowadays, the dish might seem a bit pretentious. It's certainly not the kind of thing you'd find on the menu at Bette's Diner. But never mind. It's actually quite delicious, and it's so dramatic and amusing that the performance never fails to make people smile. Don't forget to dim the lights for the full effect.

This recipe comes from our own Suzette, Diner co-founder Sue Conley.

Serves 4 to 6

I recipe (16) Bette's Diner
   Crêpes cooked (page 61)
I cup freshly squeezed orange
   juice
I tablespoon orange zest

I cup butter
⅓ cup sugar
⅓ cup orange liqueur, such as
   Grand Marnier

Preheat the oven to 400°F. Fold the crêpes into quarters and arrange them, overlapping slightly, in a large, buttered ovenproof serving dish with sides at least 1½ inches high. This can be done ahead of time.

To make the sauce, combine the orange juice, orange zest, butter, and sugar in a heavy saucepan. Bring the mixture to a boil; then simmer it, stirring occasionally, for about 5 minutes, until the sauce is syrupy and slightly caramelized. Pour the hot sauce over the crêpes and place the dish in the oven. Bake for between 5 and 10 minutes until the crêpes are warmed through and the sauce is bubbling. Warm the liqueur in a small, deep saucepan.

Bring the crêpes and the warmed liqueur to the table on a metal or foil-lined tray to catch any spills. Pour the warm liqueur over the crêpes, light a long match, and carefully ignite the surface of the sauce. Serve as soon as the flames—and the applause—have subsided.

Breton Buckwheat Crêpes

The buckwheat crêpes of Brittany are heartier and a little crisper than the classic Parisian version. Both sweet and savory fillings go well with these crêpes.

Our version is made with beer and buttermilk, which complement the tanginess of the buckwheat perfectly. You can prepare it from scratch with your own ingredients or use our Buckwheat Pancake Mix as a base.

About 16 seven-inch crêpes

Version I

These are made from scratch.

3 eggs
I cup buttermilk
I cup beer.
¼ cup melted butter
⅔ cup buckwheat flour

⅔ cup all-purpose flour
2 teaspoons baking powder
¼ teaspoon baking soda
2 teaspoons sugar
¼ teaspoon salt

In a large bowl, beat the eggs. Stir in the buttermilk, beer, and melted butter. In another bowl, combine the flours, baking powder, baking soda, sugar, and salt. Add the liquid ingredients to the dry, blending well. Chill the batter for at least I hour.

Heat a crêpe pan over medium heat and wipe it with oil. Spoon in enough batter to barely cover pan, tilting the pan to coat the bottom and part way up the sides evenly. Turn the crêpe over when the edges begin to pull away from pan and the bottom is lightly browned, 1 to 2 minutes. Continue cooking to brown the other side lightly, about 30 seconds more. Remove the crêpe from the pan and repeat the process, oiling the pan as needed and stacking the cooked crêpes.

Version 2

These are made with Bette's Buckwheat Pancake mix.

3 eggs
I cup water
I cup beer

¼ cup butter, melted
1¼ cups Bette's Diner
Buckwheat Pancake Mix

In a large bowl, beat the eggs. Stir in the water, beer, and melted butter. Add the pancake mix, beating well. Chill the batter for at least I hour. To cook the crêpes, follow the directions given for Version I.

Both versions are delicious with sour cream, caviar, smoked fish, crabmeat, ham and Gruyère cheese, mushrooms, or caramelized onions.

Swedish Pancakes Erickson

You've heard of Chicken Tetrazzini? Peach Melba? These famous dishes were named for great operatic divas. We like this tradition, and we've named our Swedish pancakes after our own Diner Diva, soprano Kaaren Erickson Sooter, a longtime friend and customer whose career has included such high points as an impromptu concert at the Diner and singing lead roles at the Metropolitan Opera. This is her Uncle Oskar's traditional recipe. Kaaren remembers her mother turning these pancakes out in rapid succession while the hungry kids snatched them up and ate them with their fingers.

Swedish pancakes are also known as plättar. *They are delicate, eggy, and thin, more like a crêpe than a pancake, so we've included them in this section. Although Swedish pancakes are traditionally made in a* plättpan—*a special cast iron skillet with three-inch round depressions into which the batter is poured to make tiny, perfectly round cakes—a crêpe pan or nonstick frying pan also works well.*

About 16 seven-inch pancakes; serves 4

4 eggs	Melted butter for greasing pan
I cup milk	Confectioners' sugar
½ teaspoon sugar	Canned lingonberries or
¼ teaspoon salt	lingonberry preserves
¼ cup flour	

Place the eggs, milk, sugar, salt, and flour, in that order, in a blender. Blend at top speed for about 30 seconds. Scrape down any lumps from the side of the blender container with a rubber spatula. Blend for 15 seconds more. (If you don't have a blender, combine all the ingredients in a bowl and beat with a wire whisk or electric beater until they are well blended.) Cover and refrigerate the batter overnight or for at least I hour.

Heat a crêpe pan or nonstick frying pan over medium heat and wipe it with the melted butter. Spoon in enough batter to barely cover the pan, tilting the pan to coat the bottom and part way up the sides evenly. Turn the pancake over after I or 2 minutes. Continue cooking to brown the other side lightly, about 30 seconds more. Remove the pancake from the pan and immediately sprinkle it with confectioners' sugar. Spread about a tablespoonful of lingonberries over the surface of the pancake, and roll it tightly. Dust with a little more confectioners' sugar and eat right away. Repeat with the remaining batter.

Ham and Cheese Crêpe Gâteau

This makes an elegant first course or a nice brunch entrée. You can assemble the gâteau and make the sauce up to a day ahead of time, then bake the gâteau and reheat the sauce just before serving.

Serves 4 to 6

1 cup shredded Gruyère cheese	1 to 2 tablespoons Dijon
½ cup grated Parmesan cheese	mustard
1 recipe (16) Bette's Diner	15 very thin slices Westphalian
Crêpes, cooked (page 61)	or Black Forest ham
¼ cup butter, melted	2 cups heavy cream

Preheat the oven to 375°F. Combine the cheeses and set aside.

Place one crêpe with the best side facing up on a foil-lined baking sheet. Brush the crêpe with a small amount of butter. Spread about ¼ teaspoon mustard over the crêpe and sprinkle on a layer of the cheese mixture. Place a slice of ham over the cheese, pulling it apart slightly if necessary to cover the crêpe to the edges. Continue layering crêpes with butter, mustard, ham, and cheese until all the crêpes are used, ending with a crêpe. Brush the top of the stack with butter and bake the gâteau about 20 minutes, until the top is nicely browned.

To make the sauce, bring the cream to a rolling boil in a heavy saucepan. Reduce the heat to a gentle boil and continue to cook it for between 10 and 15 minutes, until the cream is reduced by half.

Cut the gâteau into 4 or 6 wedges. Pool 2 or 3 tablespoons of the warm sauce on each plate and place a slice of the gâteau over the sauce.

For a lighter presentation, serve with *crème fraîche* or a little Dijon mustard in place of the cream sauce.

Dairy Pancakes

We're using the term *dairy* here in the Yiddish sense, the way the Jewish dairy restaurants of New York's Lower East Side do. Dairy (or in Yiddish, *milchik*) simply refers to kosher meatless dishes (as opposed to *flaishik* dishes made with meat). Jewish dairy dishes aren't necessarily made with dairy products, though the "holy trinity" of sour cream, cottage cheese, and cream cheese tends to figure prominently.

The great dairy restaurants of New York, like Ratner's on Delancey Street, have contributed much to the American menu—especially in the way of breakfast and brunch foods— from bagels and lox to blintzes, *matzo brei*, potato *latkes*, cream herring, and knishes.

The pancakes served at these restaurants are of the Eastern European variety. At their finest, they are rich and flavorful, but also delicate and airy because they're often made with beaten egg whites and very little flour. Sour cream and fruit preserves are the classic accompaniments.

Cottage Cheese Pancakes

After chicken soup, we think these simple pancakes are the original Jewish comfort food. Serve them with plenty of sour cream and jam.

12 to 16 three-inch pancakes; serves 2 to 4

3 eggs   ¼ cup all-purpose flour
¼ teaspoon salt   ¾ cup large-curd cottage cheese

Separate the eggs. In a large bowl, beat the yolks until they are thick and pale. Add the salt, flour, and cottage cheese, stirring just to combine. In another bowl, beat the egg whites until they are stiff but not dry; fold the egg whites into the egg yolk mixture.

Heat a lightly oiled griddle or heavy skillet over medium-high heat (375°F on an electric griddle). Portion the batter by heaping tablespoonfuls onto the hot griddle, spacing them apart. When bubbles cover the surface of the pancakes and their undersides are lightly browned, turn them over and cook them for a few minutes more, until the other sides are browned.

EGG WHITES
*A rule of thumb for beating egg whites:
Their stiffness should correspond to the
consistency of the ingredients into which you
will fold them. A heavy cake batter, for example,
needs stiffer egg whites than a light,
liquid pancake batter does.*

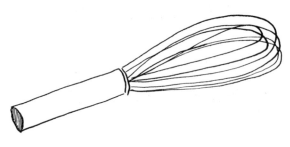

Sour Cream Cloud Cakes

*O*kay, *these are not exactly health food. But when you feel like splurging, give them a try. Or, if that makes you feel too guilty, use light sour cream instead. These are some of the lightest pancakes we've ever tasted, and they're remarkably easy to make. Serve them with maple syrup or berry preserves.*

About 24 three-inch pancakes; serves 4

4 eggs	2 teaspoons baking powder
2 cups sour cream	¼ teaspoon salt
⅔ cup all-purpose flour	

Beat the eggs lightly. Blend in the sour cream. In another bowl, combine the flour, baking powder, and salt. Add the sour cream mixture, stirring just to combine.

Heat a lightly oiled griddle or heavy skillet over medium-high heat (375°F on an electric griddle). Portion the batter by heaping tablespoonfuls onto the hot griddle, spacing them apart. When bubbles cover the surface of the pancakes and their undersides are lightly browned, turn them over and cook them for a few minutes more, until the other sides are browned.

Matzo Meal Pancakes

Matzo meal is nothing more than finely ground matzo, the thin, unleavened cracker bread served during the Passover holiday. It's used in matzo balls and gefilte fish, and it makes delicious, fluffy pancakes. You can find matzo meal in the specialty or Jewish foods section of most large supermarkets.

12 to 16 three-inch pancakes; serves 2 to 4

3 eggs   ½ teaspoon salt
½ cup matzo meal   ½ teaspoon sugar
½ cup water

Separate the eggs. In a large bowl, beat the yolks lightly. Add the matzo meal, water, salt, and sugar, and stir to combine. Beat the egg whites until they are stiff but not dry, and fold them into the yolk mixture.

Heat a lightly oiled griddle or heavy skillet over medium-high heat (375°F on an electric griddle). Portion the batter by heaping tablespoonfuls onto the hot griddle, spacing them apart. When bubbles cover the surface of the pancakes and their undersides are lightly browned, turn them over and cook them for a few minutes more, until the other sides are browned.

Golda Meir's Matzo Brei

Golda Meir, the Prime Minister of Israel from 1969 to 1974, was also, for a time, Bette's great-aunt-by-marriage. On a trip to Israel in 1971, Bette spent a memorable five days at Golda's place in Jerusalem. One morning, Golda prepared matzo brei—the best Bette had ever tasted. This is how she made it and how we make it at the Diner.

We serve Golda's matzo brei with a generous dollop of sour cream on the side, but some prefer it with jam or applesauce.

Serves 2 to 4

3 eggs
½ teaspoon salt
2 cups boiling water

4 matzos
2 tablespoons butter

Beat the eggs well in a large bowl. Add the salt. In another bowl, crumble the matzos (into pieces about 1-inch square). Pour the boiling water over the crumbled matzos, wait about 30 seconds, then drain the matzos in a colander set in the sink. Add the drained matzos to the beaten eggs, stirring to combine well.

In a 10-inch nonstick pan, melt the butter over medium-high heat. Add the matzo mixture, spreading it evenly across the bottom of the pan. Fry until the underside is golden brown and the mixture has formed a fairly solid mass; this will take 3 to 4 minutes. Flip the *matzo brei* in one piece, by covering the pan with a plate, inverting the *matzo brei* onto the plate and sliding it back into the pan. Cook the other side a few minutes more until it is nicely browned, the egg is just set, and the entire *matzo brei* is cooked through. Cut into wedges and serve.

Rice and Sesame Pancakes

Cooked rice and crunchy sesame seeds give these pancakes an appealing texture and a soothing flavor reminiscent of rice pudding. This is a great way to use up leftover cooked rice.

Serve with warm maple syrup, sour cream, or berry jam.

About 16 four-inch pancakes; serves 4

1½ cups all-purpose flour	I teaspoon vanilla extract
I tablespoon baking powder	⅛ teaspoon almond extract
1½ teaspoons sugar	(optional)
½ teaspoon salt	½ cup cooked rice, at room
2 eggs	temperature
2 cups milk	2 tablespoons toasted sesame
¼ cup melted butter	seeds

Combine the flour, baking powder, sugar, and salt. Separate the eggs. Combine the egg yolks, milk, butter, vanilla extract, and almond extract, if using. Stir the egg yolk mixture into the flour mixture. Fold in the rice and sesame seeds. In another bowl, beat the egg whites until they are stiff but not dry, and gently fold them into the batter.

Heat a lightly oiled griddle or heavy skillet over medium-high heat (375°F on an electric griddle). Portion the batter by ¼-cup measures onto the hot griddle, spacing them apart. When bubbles cover the surface of the pancakes and their undersides are lightly browned, turn them over and cook a few minutes more, until the other sides are browned.

Quick Pantry Pancakes

These light pancakes are the fastest and simplest to prepare in this book. You can turn them out in about five minutes, start to finish. Served with jam, fruit preserves, fresh berries, or other fruit, they make a simple, satisfying breakfast.

About 12 three-inch pancakes; serves 3 or 4

4 eggs

1 cup cottage cheese

2 tablespoons vegetable oil

½ cup quick-cooking oats

½ teaspoon baking soda

¼ teaspoon salt

Place all the ingredients in the order listed, in a blender or food processor and blend for 5 to 6 seconds.

Heat a lightly oiled griddle or heavy skillet over medium-high heat (375°F on an electric griddle). Portion the batter by heaping tablespoonfuls onto the hot griddle, spacing them apart. When bubbles cover the surface of the pancakes and their undersides are lightly browned, turn them over and cook them for a few minutes more, until the other sides are browned.

Cheese Blintzes

Blintzes are among the best-known dairy dishes, and deservedly so. Crispy and golden on the outside and warm and creamy inside, a great blintz offers deliciously contrasting textures and flavors. Blintzes aren't really pancakes, but because they're made from crêpes, we're including them.

If you've mastered crêpe making, you're ready to try blintzes, which are nothing more than crêpes that have been cooked on one side only, then wrapped around a simple sweet or savory filling, with the cooked side facing in. You can prepare the crêpes well in advance, roll the blintzes a few hours before you plan to serve them, and then brown them at the last minute.

Farmer cheese or pot cheese (drier versions of cottage cheese) are ideal for a blintz filling, though they can be hard to find. Conventional large-curd cottage cheese can also be used, but it should be drained for an hour or more in the refrigerator in a fine-mesh strainer set over a bowl. This helps the filling hold together better, and produces blintzes with a delicately firm texture. If you don't have time to drain cottage cheese, you can replace some of it with ricotta cheese as indicated below.

At the Diner, we serve blintzes with sour cream and fruit preserves (berry or cherry are best) on the side. They're also wonderful with warm Blueberry Compote Topping (page 130).

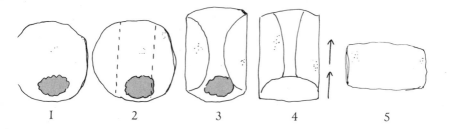

1   2   3   4   5

16 blintzes; serves 4

I recipe (16) Bette's Diner crêpes, prepared according to the
recipe on page 61, but cooked on one side only

Filling

3 cups farmer cheese or pot
cheese; *or* 3 cups large-curd
cottage cheese, drained for I
hour or more in a fine-mesh
strainer; *or* 2 cups
large-curd cottage cheese
and I cup ricotta cheese

2 egg yolks
I ½ tablespoons sugar
I ½ teaspoons freshly grated
lemon zest
I teaspoon vanilla extract
2 to 3 tablespoons butter, as
needed for browning

To make the filling, mix the cheese, egg yolks, sugar, lemon zest,
and vanilla.

To assemble blintzes, place a crêpe, cooked-side-up, on a
clean surface. Place 2 tablespoons of filling on one end of the
crêpe. Fold each side in, then roll the blintz from the bottom up,
ending with the seam-side facing down (see drawing).

Heat I tablespoon butter in a large nonstick frying pan
over medium-high heat. Place a few blintzes in the pan, seam-
sides down. Avoid crowding too many blintzes into the pan. Fry
until they are nicely browned, 3 or 4 minutes on each side,
adding more butter as needed.

Spinach Crespelle

*C*respelle *are the Italian answer to blintzes. Because we use the same basic blintz method outlined in the preceding recipe to make them, we've included them here. These* crespelle *are a popular lunch special at the Diner. They can be served with a light dusting of Parmesan cheese or a little warm tomato sauce.*

16 crespelle; serves 4 to 6

1 recipe (16) Bette's Diner Crêpes, prepared according to the recipe on page 61, but cooked on one side only

Filling

1 pound ricotta cheese
1 cup chopped cooked spinach, squeezed dry
¼ cup grated Parmesan cheese
2 tablespoons finely chopped green onions

3 tablespoons chopped toasted pecans
1 egg yolk, beaten
Pinch nutmeg
Salt and pepper to taste

Combine all the ingredients for the filling.

To assemble the *crespelle,* follow the procedure for Cheese Blintzes on page 81.

Sourdough Pancakes

*I*n the evolution of bread baking, sourdough pancakes are the link between ancient unleavened flatbreads and modern yeasted breads. More than five thousand years ago, some unsuspecting Egyptian baker discovered that flour and water, left out in the open air overnight, began to froth and bubble, and that breads baked from this dough rose higher and had a lighter texture than unleavened breads did. What this lucky baker had discovered was the process of using "wild," airborne yeast—which converts starches and sugars into carbon dioxide gas—as a leavening agent.

Bakers eventually learned that the sour mixture could be kept alive indefinitely by "feeding" it more flour and water, so that a small bit of this starter could be used to leaven more bread. And from that time until the introduction of commercial powdered yeast in the nineteenth century, yeast starters or sponges were the leavening agents used in bread baking.

Today, some starters are alleged to be centuries old, and are highly prized for their distinctive flavor. Others—like the world famous sourdough of San Francisco—are said to benefit from a strain of special airborne yeast particular to the area.

Those yeasts add something special to our fluffy sourdough pancakes and waffles, across the Bay at the Diner, too. When we decided to put them on our menu as a regular weekly pancake special, we borrowed a bit of "mother sponge" from Steve and Susie Sullivan at Berkeley's famous Acme Bakery up the street and we've been using this same wonderful starter for years.

Bette's Diner Sourdough Pancakes

These are delicious with maple syrup and a side of ham and eggs. Note that the starter needs time to compose itself—about eight hours or, perhaps more conveniently, overnight—before it can be used in a recipe.

About 24 four-inch pancakes; serves 4

2 cups sourdough starter (see page 88)
2 cups milk
2 cups all-purpose flour
2 eggs, beaten

2 tablespoons sugar
2 teaspoons baking soda
½ teaspoon salt
2 tablespoons melted butter

The night before, add the milk and flour to the starter. Place half of this mixture in a bowl, cover it with plastic wrap, and return it to the refrigerator; your starter is now replenished and will last up to 2 weeks.

Place the other half of the mixture in a loosely covered bowl (covering the bowl with a plate or towel works well) in a warm place, between 70° and 75°, for about 8 hours.

In the morning, add the eggs, sugar, baking soda, salt, and melted butter. Let the batter sit for about 10 minutes. Heat a lightly oiled griddle or heavy skillet over medium-high heat (375°F on an electric griddle). Portion ¼-cup measures of batter onto the hot griddle, spacing them apart. When bubbles cover the surface of the pancakes and their undersides are lightly browned, turn them over and cook them for about 2 minutes more, until the other sides are browned.

Sourdough Waffles

Without any modifications, this recipe makes outstanding waffles. For an extra-light, crispy waffle, you can separate the eggs and beat the whites until they are stiff but not dry, then prepare the batter as directed, folding in the whites last. Pour about ½ to ¾ cup of batter (check the manufacturer's directions) onto the hot waffle iron, close the lid, and bake the waffle until it stops steaming and is nicely browned.

Quick Sourdough Starter

If you don't already happen to have a sourdough sponge made from airborne yeast, here's a simple way to make sourdough starter from scratch using active dry yeast.

Makes 2 cups

I cup warm water (about 90°F)   I cup flour
I packet (2½ teaspoons) active
   dry yeast

In a bowl, combine the water and yeast. Whisk in the flour, leaving the mixture slightly lumpy. Cover the bowl and let it sit in a warm place, between 70°and 75°F, for 8 hours or until it begins to bubble and smell slightly sour. You should have about 2 cups of starter.

Your starter is now ready to use or you can cover and refrigerate it for up to 2 weeks.

After 2 weeks, the starter will become rancid unless it is replenished. To replenish it, simply make a batch of sourdough pancakes as directed in the preceding recipe (in which half the starter is used and the other half replenished); or discard half the starter and add I cup milk and I cup flour to the remainder.

Before replenishing or using a starter, always bring it to room temperature. If it develops a pinkish color or a strong, acrid aroma, discard it.

English Muffins

The English muffin is really the American cousin of the British crumpet. Both are related to the pancake because they are baked on a flat-topped griddle. Crumpet batter is thin and liquid, and must be baked in crumpet rings—small metal ring molds that keep the batter from spreading on the griddle. English muffins are made from a stiffer dough that is kneaded to develop the gluten in the flour. The result is an airy pancake-bread filled with tiny cavities for butter and jam to lodge in.

Our English muffins, leavened with sourdough starter, have a slightly tangy flavor and a delicate crumb.

8 three-inch muffins

½ cup sourdough starter   2 tablespoons sugar
  (see page 88)   ½ teaspoon baking soda
About 3 cups all-purpose flour   ½ teaspoon salt
I cup milk   Cornmeal, for dusting

In a large bowl, combine the starter, 2 cups of the flour, and the milk. Cover the bowl loosely and let it sit in a warm place, between 70° and 75°F, overnight or for about 8 hours.

Add the milk, sugar, baking soda, and salt, stirring vigorously until the ingredients are well combined. Turn the dough out onto a well-floured board and knead it lightly for 3 to 5 minutes, adding up to I cup of flour until the dough loses its stickiness.

Roll out the dough ¾-inch thick and cut circles with a 3-inch cookie cutter (or use the open end of a large tuna can). Sprinkle both sides of each dough circle with cornmeal, and place the circles on an ungreased cookie sheet. Cover the muffins with a cloth and set them aside in a warm place for an hour or until the dough rises, doubling in size.

Heat a lightly oiled griddle or heavy skillet over medium-high heat (about 375°F on an electric griddle). Cook the muffins for about 5 minutes on each side. Like pancakes, English muffins should be turned only once.

Cool the muffins on a rack. Split them with a fork, toast them, and serve them with butter and jam.

Oven Pancakes

*P*ancakes baked in the oven are dramatic and impressive. They're also surprisingly easy to throw together, and don't require you to stand guard over a hot griddle, because most or all of the cooking takes place in the oven or under the broiler.

Following are two of our favorite types of oven pancakes: the slightly more elaborate soufflé pancake made with beaten egg whites, and the simple yet spectacular Dutch Bunny.

Bette's Diner Soufflé Pancake

*T*his is the show-stopper of our breakfast menu. We've been serving these soufflé pancakes since we opened the Diner, and they've become a signature dish that people tell their friends about and order week after week.

Traditionally, soufflés are made with a béchamel (white sauce) enriched with egg yolks and lightened with beaten egg whites. To fit the rapid pace of short-order cooking, we developed this speedy pan soufflé, which starts on the stove top and is finished under the broiler. In the early years of the Diner, we served two flavors, Banana-Rum and Apple-Brandy; over the years, we've added a variety of savory and dessert versions, all based on the same versatile batter and cooking method. You'll find some of our favorites after the recipe for the soufflé pancake base that follows.

When these pancakes are removed from the broiler, they are beautifully puffed and browned. You'll need to watch carefully during the last few minutes of cooking to make sure that the soufflé doesn't get overcooked. An overcooked soufflé will fall immediately; one that is perfectly cooked will stay high and puffy all the way to the table. As the pancake cools, the center will continue to cook. Instruct your guests on the proper way to eat a soufflé pancake: edges first, center last.

Soufflé Pancake Base

I eight-inch pancake; serves I or 2

3 eggs	½ teaspoon sugar
½ cup half-and-half	1½ tablespoons butter, melted
¼ cup all-purpose flour	

Preheat the broiler.

    Separate the eggs and set the whites aside. Beat *two* of the egg yolks with the half-and-half (reserve the third yolk for another purpose). Add the flour slowly, stirring just to combine. Stir in the sugar, salt, and melted butter. (At this point, add to the batter those ingredients specified in your chosen recipe.) Beat the egg whites until they form soft peaks. Fold the egg whites into batter.

    Heat a lightly greased ten-inch nonstick frying pan with an ovenproof handle or a heavy cast-iron skillet until it is almost smoking. Pour the batter into the pan. Reduce the heat to medium and cook until the bottom of the pancake is nicely browned and the batter has begun to firm up, about 5 minutes.

(Arrange the pieces of prepared fruit, nuts or other ingredients called for in your chosen recipe in a circular pattern on top of the batter, laying them gently on the surface.) Place the pan between 4 and 5 inches below the broiler and cook until the top of the pancake is brown and the center is just set but still soft.

Gently slide the pancake onto a warmed serving plate, dust the fruit and dessert varieties with confectioners' sugar, and whisk it to the table. Serve immediately with butter and warm maple syrup or other toppings, as indicated in your chosen recipe.

MELTING BUTTER
When preparing the batter for soufflé
pancakes, melt the butter right in
the skillet you'll be using to make
the pancakes. This saves you the step
of greasing the skillet later.

Fruit Soufflé Pancakes

Apple-Brandy

To the batter, add 1 tablespoon applejack, Calvados, or other brandy. Top the half-cooked pancake with sautéed apples just before placing it under the broiler.

For sautéed apples: Heat 1 tablespoon butter in a small frying pan. Add 1 cup peeled, cored, sliced apple (1 medium apple) and ¼ teaspoon cinnamon. Sauté over medium heat until just soft.

Banana-Rum

To the batter, add 1 tablespoon dark rum. Top the half-cooked pancake with 1 cup sliced banana (1 large banana) just before placing it under the broiler. Dust with confectioners' sugar before serving.

Fresh Berry and Grand Marnier

To the batter, add 1 tablespoon Grand Marnier liqueur. Toss 1 cup fresh blueberries, blackberries, raspberries, or sliced strawberries, or a combination of any of these, with 1 tablespoon sugar. Stir the berries into the batter, reserving a few to place on top of the half-cooked pancake before it goes under the broiler. Dust with confectioners' sugar before serving.

Dessert Soufflé Pancakes

Chocolate

To the batter, add 2 tablespoons prepared chocolate syrup, ¼ cup chocolate chips, and 2 tablespoons dark rum (optional). Sprinkle the half-cooked pancake with a few additional chocolate chips just before placing it under the broiler. Dust with confectioners' sugar before serving.

Nutty Praline

Bring 2 tablespoons sugar, 2 tablespoons water, and a few drops of lemon juice to a boil in the pan you will be using for the pancake. Continue to boil until the sugar is lightly caramelized, about 4 minutes. Stir in ¼ cup chopped pecans. Cook 1 minute more and remove from heat. Reserve a few pecans for garnish. Prepare the batter as directed, adding 2 tablespoons dark rum. Pour the batter over the pecans in the pan. Sprinkle the reserved pecans over the half-cooked pancake just before placing it under the broiler. Dust with confectioners' sugar and serve with maple syrup or warm caramel sauce.

Grand Marnier

To the batter, add 3 tablespoons Grand Marnier or other orange liqueur. Sprinkle the top of the half-cooked pancake with 2 teaspoons sugar just before it goes under the broiler. Dust with confectioners' sugar and serve with ice cream or vanilla-flavored whipped cream.

CARAMELIZING SUGAR
When caramelizing sugar, add a few drops of lemon juice to keep the sugar from crystallizing.

Savory Soufflé Pancakes

To make wonderful savory soufflé pancakes that are perfect for brunch or a light dinner, substitute ½ teaspoon dry mustard for the sugar in the base recipe on page ooo. Add a pinch of cayenne pepper to the batter for a little extra flavor. These savory variations cook faster than the sweet versions and only need about 3 minutes under the broiler. Watch carefully to avoid overcooking.

Chile-Cheese

To the batter, add ½ cup grated Cheddar, Monterey Jack, or Swiss cheese and ½ cup diced, peeled, roasted fresh *pasilla* chiles, red bell peppers, or Anaheim chiles (see box). Reserve a few of the diced chiles to sprinkle over the half-cooked pancake just before placing it under the broiler.

Crab and Avocado

To the batter, add ½ cup cooked crabmeat and ½ ripe avocado cut into ½-inch chunks.

Green Onion and Bacon

Cook, drain, and crumble 3 strips bacon. To the batter add the crumbled bacon and ¼ cup thinly sliced green onions.

Ham and Cheese

To the batter, add ½ cup grated Gruyère or Cheddar cheese. Sprinkle the half-cooked pancake with ¼ cup diced ham just before it goes under the broiler.

ROASTING PEPPERS

*Put whole chile peppers or bell peppers in an
ovenproof pan and broil them, turning them
occasionally, until they are charred all over.
You may also char the peppers over the
burner of a gas stove or over hot coals
in a barbecue. Transfer the charred peppers
to a heavy plastic or paper bag and
seal it tightly. After about 20 minutes,
the charred skin can easily be peeled off.*

Dutch Bunny

*T*he Dutch Bunny is a minor miracle. It's really nothing more than eggs, milk, butter, and flour baked in a hot oven. But if you've never made one, you're in for a surprise. The thin, liquid batter—much like popover or Yorkshire pudding batter—cooks quickly, producing lots of steam, and the result is an enormously puffed pancake with crusty brown edges, a soft, eggy center, and a rich and buttery flavor.

There's really nothing Dutch (or, for that matter, bunnylike) about Dutch Bunnies. In fact, they were brought to America by early German settlers. Their name is probably a corruption of deutsch and possibly Pfanne, the German word for pan. The traditional German version is made with apples, and we've provided that variation as well.

A Dutch Bunny makes a nice finish to a light brunch. It's also fun to serve as a late evening snack (we recommend it with champagne on New Year's Eve) and it's just the thing to whip up for unexpected guests. Few recipes this simple deliver such stunning results from such basic ingredients.

Serves 2 to 4

3 eggs	½ cup butter, melted
¾ cups milk	Juice of ½ lemon
¾ cup all-purpose flour	Confectioners' sugar
½ teaspoon salt	

Preheat the oven to 450°F. Beat the eggs and milk until they are well blended. Add the flour and salt all at once, stirring just to combine. The batter will be slightly lumpy.

Melt the butter in a 12-inch skillet with an ovenproof handle or in a 9-by-13-inch oval baking dish. When the butter is very hot, pour in the batter, transfer the pan to the oven, and bake for 20 minutes or until the pancake is golden brown and puffed.

Assemble the guests and bring the pancake to the table immediately (the pancake will begin to deflate quickly). Sprinkle the pancake with lemon juice and confectioners' sugar. Cut into wedges; serve with maple syrup or fruit preserves (apricot is particularly good).

German Apple Pancake

Peel, core and slice 2 tart apples. Toss with 3 tablespoons sugar, 2 tablespoons lemon juice, and ¼ teaspoon cinnamon. Melt 2 tablespoons butter in a heavy skillet or sauté pan. Sauté the apples in the butter until just soft. Prepare Dutch Bunny batter. Heat 4 tablespoons butter in a skillet or oval baking dish as directed in the Dutch Bunny recipe. Spread the apples in the bottom of the skillet or dish. Pour the batter over the sautéed apples and transfer the pan to the oven. Bake about 20 minutes. Sprinkle with lemon juice and dust with confectioners' sugar.

Dutch Babies

Divide either of the recipes above among four 6-inch pans. Bake for about 15 minutes.

*P*otatoes are a cornerstone of the American diner menu, and Bette's is a case in point. Our customers can't seem to get enough of them. Every week, we turn a monumental one thousand pounds of potatoes into home fries, potato salad, corned beef hash, and, of course, potato pancakes.

Grated, shredded, puréed, or mashed, potatoes make wonderful, crispy pancakes. And potatoes are one of the great nutritional bargains because they're low in calories (a medium potato has about 110 calories) and rich in vitamin C and complex carbohydrates.

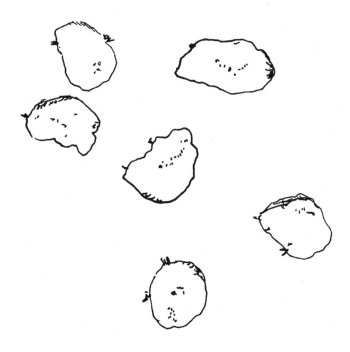

Bette's Diner Potato Pancakes

Bette's husband, Manfred, grew up on a small family farm outside Hamburg, Germany. For Sunday dinner, his mother, Ursula, would prepare red cabbage and pork chops, served with Kartoffelpuffer—golden brown, crispy potato pancakes. Her simple recipe has been a signature dish at the Diner from the day we opened.

We grate our potatoes to order for these pancakes so they're always fresh-tasting and crisp. We serve them for breakfast with homemade applesauce and sour cream, or as a lunch special with grilled bockwurst and applesauce.

About 12 four-inch pancakes; serves 4

2 eggs, beaten
¼ cup all-purpose flour
¼ cup grated onion
1 teaspoon salt
½ teaspoon pepper

4 medium russet potatoes
  (about 8 ounces each),
  peeled and shredded using
  the largest holes of a hand
  grater
¼ cup vegetable oil

Combine the eggs, flour, onion, salt, and pepper, stirring to blend. Using your hands, squeeze out as much liquid as you can from the potatoes. Add the potatoes to the egg mixture, mixing well.

In a large, heavy skillet, heat some of the oil over medium-high heat. Spoon the batter by quarter-cupfuls onto the hot skillet, flattening them with the back of the spoon. Fry until the bottom of the pancakes are nicely browned — between 3 and 5 minutes; flip the pancakes and cook for about 3 minutes longer. Repeat for the remaining pancakes, adding oil to the skillet as needed.

Drain on paper towels and serve immediately.

Phil's Famous Potato Latkes

Potato latkes are best known as a Chanukah specialty. Like most Jewish holiday foods, latkes have symbolic value: Because they are fried in oil, they are a reminder of the first Chanukah oil lamp, the menorah, which is said to have burned miraculously for eight days.

This recipe comes from a long-time customer of the Diner, Philip Siegelman, for whom latkes are somewhere between a science and a religious calling. After years of experimentation, he hit upon the rather unorthodox idea of adding a small amount of grated cheese to the batter, an innovation that doesn't much affect the flavor of the pancakes, but gives them a surprisingly crispy texture and beautiful golden brown color. (Purists may omit the cheese—the results are still outstanding.)

Because potatoes vary in size and water content, you'll need to adjust the amount of flour you use. The batter should be fairly liquid, about the consistency of chunky applesauce.

Use high-quality, fresh oil and make sure it is always hot enough before adding the batter. This will make the difference between light, crispy latkes and soggy, greasy ones.

About 12 latkes; serves 2 to 4

2 medium russet potatoes (about 8 ounces each), peeled	1 teaspoon baking powder
½ large onion	½ teaspoon salt
1 egg, lightly beaten	2 tablespoons shredded Swiss or Jack cheese (optional)
¼ to ½ cup all-purpose flour	¼ to ½ cup vegetable oil

Grate the potatoes and onion into a large bowl, using the medium-fine holes of a hand grater to produce a pulpy mush. Add the egg, ¼ cup of the flour, the baking powder, salt, and cheese, stirring to just to combine. If the batter looks too thin, add up to ¼ cup more flour.

Pour enough oil into a heavy skillet or sauté pan to cover the bottom of the pan to a depth of about ¼ inch; heat the oil over medium-high heat. Test the temperature by dropping a teaspoon of the batter into the oil; it should sizzle immediately and begin to brown after 30 seconds. Spoon the batter by scant quarter-cupfuls into the skillet, pressing the pancakes down gently to make them flat and round. Fry until the edges look crisp and the undersides are nicely browned; flip and cook them for a few minutes longer. Repeat for the remaining pancakes, adding oil to the skillet as needed.

Drain the pancakes on paper towels and serve them immediately, or place them on a cookie sheet between layers of paper towels and keep them warm in a 250°F oven, for up to 15 minutes. Serve with sour cream and applesauce.

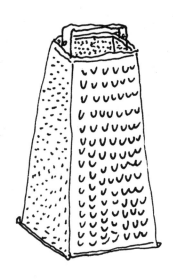

Peg Smith's Wild Mushroom Potato Pancake

*T*his *mushroom-filled potato pancake, served in wedges as a side dish, is a variation on the Straw Potato Cake served at Berkeley's legendary restaurant, Chez Panisse. The recipe comes from Peg Smith, who has cooked there for thirteen years and now heads the upstairs café kitchen. Back in the early days of the Diner, Peg took a few weeks off to teach our cooks the fine points of egg flipping, omelette folding, and pancake making.*

I ten-inch pancake; serves 2 to 4

2 medium russet potatoes
   (about 8 ounces each),
   peeled
¼ cup clarified butter (see box)
½ cup *chanterelles* or other wild
   mushrooms, sliced thin

2 tablespoons minced red onion
½ teaspoon chopped fresh
   thyme
Salt and pepper to taste
I tablespoon minced garlic
I teaspoon lemon juice

Grate the potatoes, using the large holes of a hand grater, to make about 2 cups. Place the grated potatoes in a large bowl and cover them with water. Let them sit for a few minutes to draw out some of their starch.

Heat 2 tablespoons of the clarified butter in a sauté pan or heavy skillet over high heat. Add the mushrooms and sauté them for a few minutes until soft. Add the onion, thyme, salt, and pepper; sauté a few minutes more. Add the garlic and lemon juice, and turn off the heat, allowing the garlic to continue cooking in the hot pan for a minute longer. Transfer the mixture to a bowl and set it aside.

Carefully lift the grated potatoes from the water, leaving the starch at the bottom of the bowl. Dry the potatoes in a lettuce spinner.

Heat the remaining 2 tablespoons of clarified butter in a 10-inch nonstick frying pan or skillet over medium-high heat. Spoon half of the potatoes into the pan in an even layer. Sprinkle the potatoes with salt and pepper and spread the mushroom mixture evenly over them. Sprinkle with a little more salt and pepper and spoon the remaining potatoes on top. Press the pancake down with a spatula and turn the heat down to medium-low. When the bottom is browned, flip the pancake by inverting it onto a plate and sliding it back into the pan. When the second side of the pancake is brown, turn it out onto a cutting board and slice it into 6 wedges. Serve immediately, or keep it warm in a 250°F oven for up to 15 minutes.

CLARIFYING BUTTER

Clarified butter allows you to cook foods at higher temperatures than ordinary butter does because the milk solids have been removed. To make ¼ cup of clarified butter, melt ⅓ cup unsalted butter over low heat in a heavy saucepan. Remove the pan from the heat. Skim off and discard the foamy solids that have risen to the top of the butter. Gently skim or pour off the clear yellow liquid into a bowl or jar (this is the clarified butter), leaving the milky, semisolid residue at the bottom of the pan. Discard this residue. Clarified butter can be kept for several months in a covered container in the refrigerator.

Irish Boxty

Boxty on the griddle,
Boxty in the pan.
If you can't make boxty,
You'll never get a man.

So goes the old folk poem about this unusual dish from the Northern Irish county of Donegal. (In the Northern California town of Berkeley, we change the last word to "domestic partner.")

Traditionally served on All Hallows' Eve, boxty falls somewhere between pancakes and scones on the quick-bread spectrum. Boxty dough can be baked as a round bread and divided into four wedges called farls, or it can be thinned with milk and lightened with baking powder, as in our recipe, and fried as pancakes on a griddle.

Our version is a little lighter and more contemporary than those made from traditional Irish recipes and makes a fine side dish for a fall or winter dinner.

About 12 three-inch pancakes; serves 4

2 eggs
1 cup mashed potatoes
¼ cup milk
2 tablespoons melted butter
½ cup all-purpose flour
2 teaspoons baking powder

½ teaspoon caraway seeds
Salt and pepper, to taste
1 uncooked russet potato,
  about 8 ounces, peeled
Butter, for frying

Beat the eggs lightly in a large bowl. Add the mashed potatoes, milk, melted butter, flour, baking powder, caraway seeds, salt, and pepper, stirring just to combine. Using the large holes of a hand grater, grate the uncooked potato directly into the bowl. Stir to combine.

In a large, heavy skillet, heat some of the butter over medium heat. Drop the batter by scant quarter-cupfuls onto the skillet, flattening it to form round pancakes. Fry for about 3 minutes on each side, until the pancakes are nicely browned. Repeat with the remaining batter, adding butter to the skillet as needed.

Pancakes on the Side

*T*he next time you're looking for an interesting side dish to round out a menu, consider a savory pancake. At the Diner, we love to turn all kinds of traditional side-dish ingredients—from grated vegetables to grains such as rice and grits—into special side-dish pancakes.

Two or three savory pancakes, topped with a simple garnish, perhaps salsa and sour cream, also make an elegant first course. Or make them the size of silver dollars, top them with a bit of something extravagant, like caviar or smoked trout, and serve them as hand-held hors d'oeuvres.

"Stamp and Go" Salt-Cod Pancakes

Niloufer Ichaporia is a force of nature. A native of Bombay, who now lives in San Francisco, she is an authority on Indian ingredients and cooking, and an entrepreneur who supplies the local restaurant community with everything from home-cured salmon to her own special skin cream formulated especially for cooks.

Occasionally, in our catering kitchen, we host informal cooking classes for Bay Area cooks. When Niloufer is teaching, you can count on all kinds of wonderful and fascinating surprises. Her elegantly accented English, her gentle charm, and her excitement about cooking as a great experiment are irresistible.

These salt cod pancakes are delicately puffed and have a beautiful golden color. They require a little extra preparation—the dried fish must be soaked overnight—but they're well worth the trouble. If you've never cooked with salt-cod, don't be intimidated. Although it may start out looking like a fossil and smelling a bit like a dog, once soaked, puréed, and cooked, it becomes creamy and delicate.

"I love these pancakes with a fruity relish," says Niloufer. "Try chopped ripe or hard green mangos with tamarind or lime, chili powder, and salt. If mangos aren't available, do the same with pineapple. If pineapples aren't handy and tomatoes are, dice them up with cucumber, a little onion, green chili, and cilantro and dress with a little olive oil, lime juice, and salt.

About 8 three-inch pancakes; serves 2 to 4

12 ounces dried, boneless salt cod	2 eggs
½ medium onion	2 tablespoons olive oil
1 to 2 fresh green jalapeño peppers, seeded	½ cup all-purpose flour
1 medium clove garlic	½ teaspoon baking powder
	1 to 2 tablespoons vegetable oil, for frying

Put the cod in a large bowl, cover it with water, and leave it to soak in the refrigerator overnight, changing the water once. Rinse the cod thoroughly, then put it in a saucepan, cover it with water, and let it simmer over heat, uncovered, for about 15 minutes. Drain and let cool slightly. Break up the cod and carefully pick out any small bones. Rinse the cod in a fine strainer under cold water. Drain well. You should have about 1 cup of cod.

Put the cod in the bowl of a food processor with the onion, jalapeño peppers, garlic, eggs, olive oil, flour, and baking powder. Process to form a smooth paste. (For a rougher texture, chop the onions and jalapeños by hand.) The recipe may be prepared up to this point several hours in advance.

In a large, heavy skillet, heat a small amount of the vegetable oil over medium-high heat. Spoon the batter by heaping tablespoonfuls onto the skillet, flattening it to form round cakes. Fry until nicely browned and slightly puffed, about 3 minutes on each side. Repeat with the remaining batter, adding oil to the skillet as needed.

Martin Yan's Green Onion Pancakes

A man of unending energy, generosity, and good humor, the Bay Area's Martin Yan has introduced millions of Americans to Asian cooking techniques and ingredients as the host of public television's "Yan Can Cook" show.

Here is Martin's recipe for what we like to call "Yancakes," from A Wok for all Seasons by Martin Yan (New York: Doubleday, 1988, reprinted by permission). We serve them at home with soy sauce, white vinegar, and Chinese mustard as condiments on the side.

∎

About 8 five-inch pancakes; serves 4

3 eggs
I teaspoon sugar
I teaspoon sesame oil
¾ teaspoon salt

¼ teaspoon white pepper
¾ cup water
I½ cups all-purpose flour
2 green onions, thinly sliced
Cooking oil

Combine the eggs, sugar, sesame oil, salt, pepper, and water in a bowl; whisk until the ingredients are evenly blended. Add the flour; whisk until smooth. Stir in the green onions.

Place a wide frying pan with a nonstick finish over medium heat until it is hot. Add a small amount of the oil, swirling to coat the surface of the pan. For each pancake, pour ⅓ cup batter into the pan and spread the batter into a 5-inch circle. Cook for 4 minutes or until the top of the pancake is dry and the bottom is golden brown; turn the pancake to brown the other side lightly. Remove the pancake and keep it warm while cooking the remaining pancakes.

Muttie's Apple Pushers

These old-fashioned apple fritters are a family favorite of our friend Helen Gustafson, a Berkeley cookbook author, tea-buyer, lecturer, and long-time fixture of the local restaurant scene.

Helen remembers how her Pennsylvania-Dutch grandmother, "Muttie," would spear the tines of a three-pronged cooking fork through the hole in the apple rings, dip them in the simple batter, fry them in bacon fat, and serve them up with heaping portions of ham and German fried potatoes. They also make a nice accompaniment to roast chicken, turkey, or pork.

About 16 fritters; serves 2 to 4

2 tablespoons sugar
2 teaspoons cinnamon
1/4 cup all-purpose flour
1 teaspoon baking powder
1/4 teaspoon salt
2 tablespoons milk

2 eggs, separated
2 medium apples, peeled, cored, and sliced into 1/4-inch rings
1 to 2 tablespoons butter, for frying

In a small bowl, combine the cinnamon and sugar, then set the mixture aside.

In a medium bowl, combine the flour, baking powder, and salt. Stir in the milk and the 2 egg yolks to form a thick batter. In another bowl, beat the egg whites until they form soft peaks. Gently fold the beaten whites into the batter with a few quick strokes.

Melt a small amount of the butter in a skillet or nonstick frying pay over medium-high heat until it begins to foam. Using the tines of a long fork, dip each apple ring into the batter, coating it completely. Transfer the apples to the frying pan, and fry for about 2 minutes. When the undersides are nicely brown, flip the fritters and fry for a few minutes more. Repeat with the remaining apples, adding more butter as necessary.

Sprinkle the fritters with the cinnamon sugar, to taste.

Garlic-Cheese Grits Cakes

A Southern specialty, these flavorful grits cakes are a wonderful accompaniment to braised meats or stewed vegetables. They also make a hearty side dish for an egg breakfast—more interesting than the usual plain grits with butter.

About 20 two-inch cakes; serves 4 to 6

2 cups unseasoned, warm, cooked grits

1 cup shredded sharp Cheddar cheese

2 tablespoons freshly grated Parmesan cheese

2 tablespoons butter

1 tablespoon minced garlic

2 tablespoons chopped green onion

1 teaspoon Worcestershire sauce

1 teaspoon salt

½ cup bread crumbs

Vegetable oil, for frying

In a large bowl, combine all the ingredients except the bread crumbs and the vegetable oil. Form the mixture into 20 patties, two inches in diameter. Roll the patties in the bread crumbs and set them on a cookie sheet lined with waxed paper. Cover with plastic wrap and refrigerate the patties for at least 30 minutes (or up to 6 hours).

In a large, heavy skillet, heat some of the oil over medium heat. Fry the patties until they are nicely browned, about 3 minutes on each side, adding oil to the skillet as needed.

Mashed Carrot Cakes

Carrot cakes and fritters are another Southern tradition. Our version is particularly light and comforting, adding a nice touch of color and sweetness to the plate. The sugar in the carrots becomes lightly caramelized as these pancakes brown, and they acquire a rich flavor and a delicately crispy exterior.

This recipe can also be used with other cooked, mashed vegetables such as acorn squash and parsnips, to make side-dish pancakes. Simply adjust the amount of flour to make a smooth batter that holds together when cooked.

About 12 pancakes; serves 4

2 eggs, lightly beaten
3 cups mashed, cooked carrots,
   at room temperature
¼ cup butter, softened

¼ to ½ cup all-purpose flour
2 teaspoons baking powder
½ cup milk
Vegetable oil, for frying

In a large bowl, combine the eggs, carrots, butter, ¼ cup of the flour, the baking soda, and the milk. The batter should be about the consistency of thick applesauce. If it is too liquid, add up to ¼ cup more flour.

In a large, heavy skillet, heat some of the oil over medium heat. Drop the batter by quarter-cupfuls onto the skillet, flattening it to form round pancakes. Fry until the pancakes are nicely browned, about 3 minutes on each side. Repeat with the remaining batter, adding oil to the skillet as needed.

Wild Rice and Pecan Pancakes

These simple cakes have an earthy, nutty flavor and an appealingly crunchy texture. Try them with roasted chicken or turkey and homemade cranberry sauce.

About 8 pancakes; serves 4

2 eggs, lightly beaten
½ cup finely chopped pecans
2 tablespoons all-purpose flour
I teaspoon baking soda
½ cup buttermilk
½ teaspoon salt
¼ teaspoon pepper

I cup cooked white rice, cooled
   to room temperature
I cup cooked wild rice, cooled
   to room temperature
2 tablespoons minced green
   onions
2 teaspoons minced garlic
Vegetable oil, for frying

In a large bowl, combine the eggs, pecans, flour, baking soda, buttermilk, salt, and pepper. Add the white rice and wild rice, the onions, and the garlic, stirring to combine.

In a large, heavy skillet, heat some of the oil over medium heat. Drop the batter by quarter-cupfuls onto the skillet, flattening it to form round pancakes. Fry until the pancakes are nicely browned, about 3 minutes on each side. Repeat with the remaining batter, adding oil to the skillet as needed.

Kidcakes

*P*ancakes have always been particularly popular with our younger customers. Here are a few simple ideas to try on yours.

Use our basic buttermilk pancake recipe (page 34), which yields about 24 four-inch pancakes, or any of our pancake mixes.

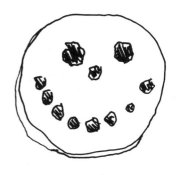

Mickey Mouse Pancakes

Pour enough batter onto the griddle to make a normal-sized pancake; immediately ladle 2 more tiny circles of batter so that they attach themselves to the first pancake to make mouse ears. Before serving, place raisins on each pancake to make the eyes and nose and a strawberry slice for the mouth.

Snowman Pancakes

Using the same technique described for Mickey Mouse Pancakes, make 3 circles, each slightly smaller than the one before. Use raisins or currants to make a face and buttons.

Alphabet Pancakes

Make pancakes shaped like letters to spell out names or initials. Remember: The letters need to be poured onto the griddle in mirror writing, so that they will read right when the pancakes are flipped.

Pineapple Upside-Down Cakes

Place a pineapple ring on the griddle. Put a cherry in the center of the ring. Ladle ¼ cup pancake batter over the pineapple; cook as directed for buttermilk pancakes.

Granola Griddle Cakes

Sprinkle a little granola into pancake batter for added crunch and sweetness.

Silver Dollar Pancakes

Kids seem to be fascinated by miniature food. Use 1 to 2 tablespoons of batter per pancake.

Pancake Sandwiches

Spread jam, jelly, or a combination of peanut butter and jelly on a cooked pancake. Top with a second pancake. Allow the sandwiches to cool slightly so that kids can eat them out of hand.

Tollhouse Cookie Pancakes

Add mini chocolate chips and chopped toasted walnuts to pancake batter before cooking it.

FREEZING PANCAKES
Pancakes and waffles can be frozen and reheated with perfectly acceptable results, so you can whip them up for hungry kids in a few minutes.
To freeze: Allow cooked pancakes or waffles to cool completely, then wrap them individually in plastic wrap or plastic bags. Reheat them in a toaster oven, a conventional oven, or a microwave oven.

Simple Pancake Toppings

New customers at Bette's Diner, and even some of our regulars, are often delighted by the unexpected extra touches we add to our plates, like an unannounced hot or cold topping with their pancakes or waffles. The same principle works well at home. Taking a few minutes to whip up a simple topping turns your favorite pancake into the special of the day.

Warm Toppings

Serve these toppings immediately, or refrigerate and reheat them before serving.

Citrus-Maple Syrup

Serves 4 to 6

¹/₂ cup pure maple syrup
¹/₂ teaspoon freshly grated
   orange or lemon zest

2 tablespoons butter or
   margarine

In a heavy saucepan, combine the syrup and zest, bring the mixture to a boil, and simmer for I minute. Stir in the butter.

Blueberry Compote Topping

Serves 4 to 6

2 cups fresh or frozen
   blueberries
¹/₂ cup orange juice
I teaspoon cornstarch
   dissolved in ¹/₄ cup water

¹/₂ teaspoon freshly grated
   orange zest
2 tablespoons sugar

In a heavy saucepan, combine the blueberries, orange juice, cornstarch mixture, zest, and sugar. Heat, stirring occasionally, until the sauce boils. Remove the pan from the heat; the sauce will thicken as it cools.

Emergency "Maple Syrup"

Serves 4 to 6

I ¹/₂ cups brown sugar
¹/₂ cup water

¹/₄ cup butter
¹/₂ teaspoon vanilla extract

Combine the sugar and water in a heavy saucepan and heat the mixture, stirring it, until the syrup comes to a boil. Remove the pan from the heat and add the butter and vanilla.

Warm Apple-Currant Topping

Serves 4 to 6

2 medium-sized tart apples, such as Granny Smith, peeled, cored, and cut into chunks

¼ cup currants
1 tablespoon brown sugar
2 teaspoons lemon juice
½ teaspoon cinnamon

In a heavy saucepan, combine the apples, currants, sugar, lemon juice, and cinnamon. Cover the pan and simmer the mixture over low heat, stirring occasionally, for between 5 and 7 minutes.

Warm Orange Sauce

Serves 4 to 6

1 tablespoon orange zest
1 cup fresh orange juice

1 cup butter
⅓ cup sugar

In a heavy saucepan, combine the orange zest and juice, butter, and sugar. Bring the mixture to a boil, reduce the heat, and simmer the sauce, stirring occasionally, for about 5 minutes or until it is syrupy.

Warm Honey "Syrup"

Honey, heated to the boiling point, will become thin and pourable, making a delicious syrup for pancakes and waffles. If desired, add a small amount of cinnamon while heating.

Cold Toppings

Cranberries and Cream

Serves 4 to 6

I can (16 ounces) whole-berry
cranberry sauce or 2 cups
homemade cranberry sauce

I cup sour cream or plain
yogurt

Combine the cranberry sauce and sour cream or yogurt, cover, and chill.

Whipped Honey Butter

Serves 4 to 6

I cup softened, unsalted butter   I cup honey

Using an electric mixer, beat the butter until it is soft and fluffy. Beat in the honey and continue beating the mixture until the ingredients are thoroughly combined.

Lemon-Poppy Seed Butter

Serves 4 to 6

I cup softened, unsalted butter
½ cup confectioners' sugar
2 teaspoons poppy seeds

I teaspoon freshly grated
lemon zest

Using an electric mixer, cream the butter and confectioners' sugar together until the mixture is light and fluffy. Beat in the poppy seeds and lemon zest and continue to beat until all the ingredients are thoroughly combined.

Any-Berry Butter

Serves 4 to 6

1 cup softened, unsalted butter
2 tablespoons confectioners'
   sugar

½ cup fresh or frozen
   raspberries, strawberries,
   or blueberries

Using an electric mixer, cream the butter and confectioners' sugar together until the mixture is light and fluffy. At low speed, blend in the berries until they are just combined in the mixture. Stir in additional confectioners' sugar if the berries are too tart.

Almond Butter

Serves 4 to 6

1 cup softened, unsalted butter
¾ cup toasted, slivered
   almonds, pulverized in a
   food processor or blender

3 tablespoons confectioners'
   sugar
Few drops almond extract

Using an electric mixer, combine the butter, pulverized almonds, confectioners' sugar, and almond extract.

About the Authors

Steve Siegelman acts as an artistic guide to the owners of Bette's Diner. He was one of the original cooks and helped develop the recipes and cooking style that made the restaurant an instant hit. Steve once heated the last tortilla in the house for James Beard and was so nervous that he burned it. Fortunately for Steve, Mr. Beard was distracted by admirers and forgot that he ever ordered it.

Sue Conley, one of the original founders of the Diner, has acted as chief cook for most of her eleven years as a hands-on owner of this lively spot. Sue once found herself seated in a white stretch limo across from Tammy Wynette, who was carefully applying pancake makeup in preparation for an appearance on "The Dolly Parton Show."

Bette Kroening is one the original founders of the Diner and the namesake of the place. These days, she spends most of her time managing the business, but her roots are in cooking. Bette once served corn cakes to Senator Jacob Javits whose daughter, Carla, worked at the Diner. Five years later, Bette almost burned down the Jacob Javits Center in New York City when she sparked an electric fire as a result of plugging in too many pancake griddles in her booth at the Fancy Food Show.

Mary Lawton poses as a Diner waitress by day but every night she draws about a town's worth of characters on her sketch pad. With wit and wisdom, Mary's nationally syndicated cartoons have appeared in such publications as *Ms.* magazine, *The Utne Reader, Bay Food,* the San Francisco *Chronicle,* and "The Diner Dish." While working as a catering chef in Boston, Mary had the privilege of delivering six dozen miniature ham and cheese crêpes personally to Julia Child for an afternoon cocktail party.

Betsy Bodine Ford is the gal responsible for the Diner's award-winning graphics. Starting with the first menu and neon sign through the design of the first edition of *The Pancake Handbook,* Betsy has served up friendly, unforgettable, sharp art from her studio in Oregon. Betsy once ate twenty-four silver dollar pancakes on a bet in Dufur, Oregon (town motto: Don't ask what Dufur can do for you, ask what you can do for Dufur.)

Enjoy your pancakes!

Bette's Diner Products

*A*ll of our pancake and scone mixes are made with all-natural, freshly milled flours. They are available in specialty food stores across the country or by mail order direct from our warehouse.

Four Grain Buttermilk Pancake and Waffle Mix: A proven hit at the Diner. Made without sugar, naturally sweet (16 ounces).

Oatmeal Pancake and Waffle Mix: Whole oats give these pancakes a nutty, sweet flavor (16 ounces).

Buckwheat Pancake and Waffle Mix: A long-standing health food, buckwheat flour gives these pancakes a distinctive, tangy flavor (16 ounces).

Raisin Scone Mix: Our original, award-winning scone mix. This mix makes moist, creamy scones every times (16 ounces).

Lemon Currant Scone Mix: The perfect scone with morning coffee, afternoon tea, or as a biscuit with dinner. Our most versatile flavor (16 ounces).

Wild Cranberry Scone Mix: Produces a sweet, wholesome scone. Dried cranberries add sparkle to this diner favorite (16 ounces).

Bette's Blend of Good, Strong Coffee: A full-bodied, aromatic brew. Available as decaf or regular (2 ounces ground or 16 ounces whole beans).

Bette's Diner Cookies: Already baked and ready to eat. We use the best ingredients available: real butter, freshly milled flours, and Arizona pecans. Bette's rich and memorable cookies come in two flavors: Double Chocolate Pecan and Butter Pecan.

For more information call (510) 601-6980 or to order by mail,

Bette's Oceanview Diner
1807A Fourth Street
Berkeley, California 94710

Index

Page numbers in boldface indicate recipes.